Edmund Burke

Series Introduction

The *Major Conservative and Libertarian Thinkers* series aims to show that there is a rigorous, scholarly tradition of social and political thought that may be broadly described as 'conservative', 'libertarian' or some combination of the two. The series aims to show that conservatism is not simply a reaction against contemporary events, nor a privileging of intuitive thought over deductive reasoning; libertarianism is not simply an apology for unfettered capitalism or an attempt to justify a misguided atomistic concept of the individual. Rather, the thinkers in this series have developed coherent intellectual positions that are grounded in empirical reality and also founded upon serious philosophical reflection on the relationship between the individual and society, how the social institutions necessary for a free society are to be established and maintained, and the implications of the limits to human knowledge and certainty.

Each volume in the series presents a thinker's ideas in an accessible and cogent manner to provide an indispensable work for both students with varying degrees of familiarity with the topic as well as more advanced scholars.

The following twenty volumes that make up the entire *Major Conservative and Libertarian Thinkers* series are written by international scholars and experts.

The Salamanca School by Andre Azevedo Alves (LSE, UK) &
    Professor José Manuel Moreira (Porto, Portugal)
Thomas Hobbes by Dr R. E. R. Bunce (Cambridge, UK)
John Locke by Professor Eric Mack (Tulane, US)
David Hume by Professor Christopher J. Berry (Glasgow, UK)
Adam Smith by Professor James Otteson (Yeshiva, US)
Edmund Burke by Professor Dennis O'Keeffe (Buckingham, UK)
Alexis de Tocqueville by Dr Alan S Kahan (Paris, France)
Herbert Spencer by Alberto Mingardi (Istituto Bruno Leoni, Italy)
Ludwig von Mises by Richard Ebeling (Trinity College)

Joseph A. Schumpeter by Professor John Medearis (Riverside, California, US)
F. A. Hayek by Dr Adam Tebble (UCL, UK)
Michael Oakeshott by Dr Edmund Neill (Oxford, UK)
Karl Popper by Dr Phil Parvin (Cambridge, UK)
Ayn Rand by Professor Mimi Gladstein (Texas, US)
Milton Friedman by Dr William Ruger (Texas State, US)
James M. Buchanan by Dr John Meadowcroft (King's College London, UK)
The Modern Papacy by Dr Samuel Gregg (Acton Institute, US)
Robert Nozick by Ralf Bader (St Andrews, UK)
Russell Kirk by Jon Pafford
Murray Rothbard by Gerard Casey

Of course, in any series of this nature, choices have to be made as to which thinkers to include and which to leave out. Two of the thinkers in the series – F. A. Hayek and James M. Buchanan – have written explicit statements rejecting the label 'conservative'. Similarly, other thinkers, such as David Hume and Karl Popper, may be more accurately described as classical liberals than either conservatives or libertarians. But these thinkers have been included because a full appreciation of this particular tradition of thought would be impossible without their inclusion; conservative and libertarian thought cannot be fully understood without some knowledge of the intellectual contributions of Hume, Hayek, Popper and Buchanan, among others. While no list of conservative and libertarian thinkers can be perfect, then, it is hoped that the volumes in this series come as close as possible to providing a comprehensive account of the key contributors to this particular tradition.

John Meadowcroft
King's College London

Edmund Burke

Dennis O'Keeffe

For the good are always the merry,
Save by an evil chance
W.B. Yeats, *The Fiddler of Dooney*

Major Conservative and Libertarian Thinkers

Series Editor: John Meadowcroft

Volume 6

BLOOMSBURY
NEW YORK • LONDON • NEW DELHI • SYDNEY

Bloomsbury Academic
An imprint of Bloomsbury Publishing Plc

175 Fifth Avenue   50 Bedford Square
New York   London
NY 10010   WC1B 3DP
USA   UK

www.bloomsbury.com

Hardback edition first published in 2010 by the Continuum International
Publishing Group Inc

This paperback edition publish by Bloomsbury Academic 2013

© Dennis O'Keeffe, 2013

Library of Congress Cataloging-in-Publication Data
A catalog record for this book is available from the Library of Congress.

ISBN: HB: 978-0-8264-2978-0
PB: 978-1-4411-9812-9

Typeset by Deanta Global Publishing Services, Chennai, India
Printed and bound in the United States of America

This book is dedicated to the memory of two young Irishmen – to my grandfather and namesake, Denis John O'Keeffe, who died aged 26 years at the Battle of Coronel, on 1 November 1914, when HMS Monmouth was lost with all hands, and to his son, my father, Patrick Joseph O'Keeffe, who died in 1942, aged 27 years.

Contents

Series Editor's Preface

Edmund Burke is today widely appreciated as one of the foremost exponents of the conservative philosophical position. But curiously for much of his life Burke was perceived to be a leading progressive and radical figure in British public life. This perception was ended, however, by his response to the French Revolution of 1789. Burke's denunciation of that revolution in his most famous work, *Reflections on the Revolution in France*, written and published as the revolution was unfolding, was founded upon a deep scepticism as to the capacity of individual reason to guide human action to beneficent results. Burke believed that social institutions could not be constructed anew each generation according to a particular generation's view of what was fair or just. Rather, social institutions were the result of an historical process of evolution often dating back many generations. Consequently, their beneficent effects may not be deductible by rational scrutiny or detached reason. It is difficult, for example, to provide a rational justification for the hereditary principle in government, but, according to a Burkean perspective, that does not mean that the hereditary principle does not perform some important function in the maintenance of social order.

Burke's great fear was that if the settled government of a society could be violently overthrown because it did not accord with a particular generation's reason, as he believed had happened in France during the revolution, then any government or social institution was liable to be destroyed if it did not happen to fit with the prevailing ideas of the day. Burke foresaw a descent into terror and chaos as different groups fought to destroy and rebuild social institutions in accordance with their own inevitably fallible ideas. In such a situation, Burke warned, 'no law be left but the will of a prevailing force'. As such, it can be argued that Burke foresaw the terror that came in the later years of the French revolution and that which was wrought by subsequent attempts to create brave new worlds in, for example, the Soviet Union, Nazi Germany and Pol Pot's Cambodia.

In this excellent volume, Professor Dennis O'Keeffe of the University of Buckingham places Burke in his historical context and carefully sets out the whole of Burke's philosophical contribution. O'Keeffe then goes on to describe Burke's reception by his contemporaries and to consider the implications of Burke's ideas for politics and policy today. No account of conservative thought would be complete without a thorough treatment of the contribution made by Burke; by presenting Burke's ideas in such an accessible and cogent form the author has made a crucial contribution to the Major Conservative and Libertarian Thinkers series.

Finally, I would like to thank Ian Hill for his editorial assistance with the preparation of this volume for publication.

John Meadowcroft
King's College London

1

Edmund Burke: The Contradictions of Benevolence

Birth and Name, Background and Religion

Edmund Burke was born in Dublin on 12 January 1729, the son of Richard Burke, a Dublin attorney, who seems to have converted to the Church of Ireland, abandoning, at least formally, his native Catholicism. Richard is a shadowy figure and his precise history is not known. But a Richard Burke did convert, or as it was called at the time, 'conform', to the Established Church in 1722, seven years before Edmund's birth. The supposition is that this was indeed Edmund's father and that the departure from the ancestral faith was made so that Richard could practise law. Such opportune conversions were at times denounced by Church of Ireland Bishops (O'Brien 1988: xxix). The religious rupture was never full, however, if indeed it possessed any substance at all, for Richard married a Catholic, Mary Nagle, from County Cork, where Nagle is one of the great names (ibid.: xxix).[1]

Burke always maintained his Catholic and Irish connections. Initially, of course, these were maintained *for* him. Edmund was sent at the age of six to Ballyduff, in County Cork, to live with his mother's brother, Patrick (McCue 1997: 13). There he attended a hedge school, an illegal Catholic open air teaching arrangement, of the kind made famous in our day by the Ulster playwright, Brian Friel.[2] Burke himself retained a lifetime interest in Irish and Irish literature (O'Brien 1997: 13).

In 1741 Edmund went to the Quaker school at Ballitore in County Kildare (Hill 1975: 11). Here he came under the loving influence of the headmaster, Abraham Shackleton, with whose son Richard he maintained a long friendship (McCue 1997: 13). Burke's profound sense of history evidently got off to an early start, as did his love of literature, since Richard later reported on Burke's delight in history and poetry. Apparently he liked the Classics too, though as 'his diversion rather than his business' (ibid.: 13).

In 1744, in his mid-teens, at an age which most people today would consider too young for higher education, Burke entered Trinity College Dublin, where Oliver Goldsmith was a fellow student (ibid.: 13). O'Brien says that young Burke's letters to Richard Shackleton are *not* marked by precocious brilliance (O'Brien 1997: 9–11). Even so, within two years he had been made 'scholar' of the House, graduating in 1748 at the age of nineteen (ibid.: 13). He had engaged in literary pursuits and debating and also organized a short-lived newspaper, *The Reformer*, which ran to thirteen issues (ibid.: 13). The title does not mean he was a headstrong or meddlesome youth. Nor does it mean that Burke was not fundamentally a conservative. As we will argue later, Burke's intelligence combines, without clash, a deep reverence for proven practice and an ever vigilant eye to the reform of abuses. For Burke, knowing what needs to be changed is of the essence of successful conservatism.

Burke moved to England two years after graduation and enrolled at the Middle Temple in 1750, with the ostensible intention of returning to Dublin to follow in his father's footsteps (Hill 1975: 11). His father having observed that Edmund's legal studies were desultory and that he was devoting himself to literature, entertainment and debating, concluded that the youth was not, after all, going to be a lawyer and duly cut off his allowance (McCue 1997: 13–14). Indeed it is difficult to conclude from subsequent events that this young man ever seriously intended to be a lawyer, despite a lifelong fascination with law and constitutionalism.

Was Burke drifting initially? Certainly, the next half decade is sometimes thought of as 'Burke's missing years' (Barkan 1972: ix). In truth, however, the years seem to have been formative ones. Elliott Barkan believes that Burke's whole philosophy took shape in this period (ibid.: ix). The publication in 1756 of *Vindication of Natural Society* and in 1757 of *On the Sublime and the Beautiful*, suggests much deep reflection. The first of these was an anonymous parody of the work of Henry St John, Viscount Bolingbroke, a deist, rationalist philosopher of the first half of the eighteenth century, who had from Burke's viewpoint traduced the state. Hill maintains that this book is important in respect of Burke's later work (Hill 1975: 12).[3]

So excellent was the satire that some contemporary hostile readers transferred their hostility to Burke when the book's true authorship was made public. This was unfortunate, since while Bolingbroke had rejected religion, the work was intended to convey Burke's quite opposite lifelong conviction that to shake the foundations of the church is also to threaten the political order and invoke anarchy (ibid.: 12). The a priori rationalism of the book – that is to say a rationalism argued from first principles, without reference to historical facts – was the kind of rootless speculation Burke always opposed (McCue 1997: 13–14). Burke refuses to be governed by abstractions. He does not, of course, deny their indispensable part in intellectual debate and politics. This would be to deny *principles,* for him indispensable to intellectual and practical coherence (Bredvold and Ross 1970: 41).

One startling twentieth-century response to *Vindication of Natural Society* is Murray Rothbard's interpretation of the work as a pioneering anarchist tract (Rothbard 1958: 114–18).[4] Genuine or satirical, however, the book is certainly innovative and in appearance deeply antinomian, that is profoundly hostile to the church and the existing political order.

The other book, whose full title is *A Philosophical Inquiry into the Origin of Our Ideas of the Sublime and Beautiful,* is an extraordinary exploration of the philosophical psychology (as we would call it today) of art and aesthetics, and one remarkable in so young an author. Jim McCue calls it 'pure philosophy' although there is a large element of what today would be called 'psychology' in it. McCue notes that it was an immediate and lasting success, running into fifteen editions in its author's lifetime (McCue 1997: 14). Such mature, indeed remarkable works, suggest lengthy pondering. It simply does not make sense to call the years that produced them 'lost'.

Ambiguity and Ambivalence, Religious and National: Jane Nugent

The religious ambiguity in Burke's family, which manifested itself in a certain religious ambivalence on Edmund's part, was one he perpetuated himself, marrying a Catholic, Jane Nugent, in 1757, having the year before taken lodgings in the London house of her Irish father, a medical doctor (ibid.: 15). Burke seemed here to be repeating his own father's complicated religious life and affiliations. It is as though Burke had singled out and occupied a little plot, representative of Ireland and its religious complications, in the London which was to prove so crucial in his life and works.

In the same year, 1757, Burke continued his labours with an extensive revision of the work by his (distant) cousin William Burke, *An Account of European Settlements in America*, a study expressing typical Burkean trust, even in lands across the oceans, in aristocracy as a responsible form of government (Barkan 1972: ix). In this work, the two Burkes express admiration for the European settlers. They emphasize the political genius of the Great Settlement of 1689 whose spirit and practice they conceive the colonists as maintaining.[5] They insist that the American colonies must enjoy freedom of trade as far as possible (Burke and Burke 1777: 182–3). In particular they appeal to a sense of kith and kin and to a common state of social development between the two societies, such development especially impressive in America. 'In no part of the world are the ordinary sort so independent, or possess so many of the conveniences of life' (ibid.: 167, 262). Juxtaposed with Burke's later more famous writings on America, this early text suggests a praiseworthy consistency in political outlook.

Preamble to Politics: *The Annual Register,* Dublin, Dr Johnson

There seems to be no definitive evidence before the late 1750s that Burke was bent on a political career. We can see why politics should have attracted his profound interest. The combination of a brilliant intellect and the seemingly intractable contradictions of religion and national background which he inherited and endured makes such an interest highly plausible. Moreover, as we have seen, at University, Burke had been active in debating and literary and academic journalism, pursuits which typically overlap with political ones. There seem to be no events and incidents, however, which we can take as definitive predictors of his later life in politics. If Barkan is right that it was between 1750 and the middle of the decade that Burke's intellectual personality took definite shape (Barkan 1972: ix), it is plausible to think that the political ambitions formed then too.

A stable married life must have helped consolidate any such ambitions. Edmund's marriage to Jane Nugent in 1757 was to prove a long and happy one. Very soon after the wedding, his younger brother Richard and collaborating 'cousin', William, had joined him in London (Hill 1975: 12). Richard and William were shortly to depart for the Caribbean. Edmund, however, seemingly making an effort to launch himself publicly, applied for but failed to obtain the consulship in Madrid (McCue 1997: 16). The work which then most occupied him, from 1758 until he went into politics proper, was the *Annual Register*, a chronicle of current politics with extensive book reviews (Hill 1975: 12). It ran until 1788, and was notable for breadth of subject matter, much of it written by Burke (McCue 1997: 14).

In 1759 Burke became Private Secretary to William Gerard Hamilton. Two years later, when Hamilton entered the service of the Lord Lieutenant of Ireland, the Earl of Halifax, Burke accompanied him to Dublin. Burke stayed with Hamilton some six years (ibid.: 16). His introduction to a notable public life came with the next round in his fortunes. On Burke's returning to London in 1764, his life took two very active turns. He had known Samuel Johnson since the 1750s. In 1764 he and his father-in-law, Dr Nugent, along with Reynolds and Goldsmith, became founder members of Johnson's club. Garrick, Sheridan, Boswell, Fox, Warton, Malone, Adam Smith and Sir William Jones joined later – all in all a startling array of talent. Even here, Burke shone (ibid.: 16).

Burke at the Centre of Politics: Tory and Whig Disarray in the 1760s

Soon after this time, in 1765, Burke became Private Secretary to the Second Marquess of Rockingham, thereby becoming a 'Rockingham' as the Marquess's followers were called (Barkan 1972: xii). His brilliance and spellbinding oratory soon made him a central policy-maker to the Whig government Rockingham formed in July 1765. In December that year, aged 36, he was duly elected Member of Parliament for Wendover (McCue 1997: 16), a seat he held till 1774 (Mitchell 1993: xxiii). According to Elliott Barkan, it had been with the assistance of William Burke that Edmund had found employment with Rockingham (Barkan 1972: xi). Moreover, William was instrumental in getting him the seat at Wendover (ibid.: x).

Rockingham's short first administration had taken office in July 1765, so Burke was at the end of the year in the Commons, in time to play a major role, establishing himself as a notable Commons speaker, and involving himself in the repeal of the Stamp Act, 1766. This act, the fourth of that name, required all legal documents, permits, business contracts, newspapers, wills, pamphlets and playing cards in the American colonies to carry a tax stamp. It was meant to offset military expenses in America and various other military expenditures. It was hugely unpopular and never properly enforced. Burke's first Parliamentary speech opposed it. The Rockinghams repealed it, though it seems improbable that Burke had very much influence (O'Brien 1997: 45).

Rockingham's government was anyway destined to fall in little more than a year, though Burke remained loyal to Rockingham till the latter's death in 1782 (McCue 1997: 17). Both major British parties were in disarray at this time, crushed by George III's anti-parliamentary policies and riven alike with internal struggle (Hill 1975: 15). At the time of Rockingham's fall, in 1766, his party did not possess a coherent outlook. Events summoned Burke to put his manifold talents into the Whig cause and he played a significant part in clarifying the Rockinghams' policies, both with regard to relations with the King and with the very agitated American colonists, menaced as they were with taxes that the Rockinghams did not support, though it was left largely to Burke to articulate their opposition (ibid.: 15). He was very active throughout the 1760s in what Barkan calls 'the tournament of factional politics' which dominated that decade (Barkan 1972: xi).

When George III, in July 1766, persuaded Pitt the Elder to form a new ministry, rewarding him with the title, Earl of Chatham, Burke asked Chatham for a position, provided he could opt out if Rockingham went into opposition. Chatham's refusal kept Burke out of power, along with Rockingham, for sixteen years (ibid.: xii). In the latter part of the 1760s Burke occupied himself splicing a Whig fragment with a Tory one to form the New Whigs and during 1769–70 he wrote their manifesto (Hill 1975: 15).

The House at Beaconsfield and *Thoughts on the Causes of Present Discontents*

In 1768 Burke had bought Gregories, a house in Beaconsfield with an extensive estate (ibid.: 18). He could not afford it – it was forever a drain – (ibid.: 18) but his intellectual production from then on was to be prodigious. The tract of 1770, *Thoughts on the Cause of Present Discontents,* aimed principally at clarifying the political purposes of the Rockinghams. It is regarded as crucial in its resistance to royal encroachment – the deliberately subversive aim of George III's policy. It is also viewed as pivotal in its adumbration of a system of permanent two-party government (Hill 1975: 16–20).[6] It thus stands at the heart of Burke's constitutional intentions for his adopted country. George's behaviour was advisedly seen as threatening the constitutional settlement of 1689.

Published in 1770, *Present Discontents* sought to contain and reverse the emasculation of Parliament. According to McCue, it was the electoral principle that was uppermost in Burke's assessments (McCue 1997: 18–19). Burke was asserting the view that the Commons answered to the people, not to the king. Burke might here be thought of as looking back as much to Cromwell and Parliament's quarrel with Charles I as forward to later constitutional clarifications in the nineteenth century. Barkan too identifies respect for the 1689 Settlement as the main historical reference point and central pillar of Burke's political outlook. He contends that Burke was 'so committed to the Settlement of 1689 and the resulting concept of Parliamentary supremacy, that he could not accept any argument questioning that principle' (Barkan 1972: xi). Such then is the sentiment which undergirds the arguments of *Present Discontents.* For our part, we might ask ourselves whether in the twenty-first century the supremacy of the Commons is being maintained to Burke's expectations:

The House of Commons can never be a control on other parts of government unless they are controlled themselves by their constituents; and unless these constituents possess some right in the choice of that House, which it is not in the power of that house to take away. (McCue 1997: 19)

Present Discontents is perhaps the crowning gem of Burke's years as Wendover's MP. The town today has glamour from its closeness to what is now Chequers, the weekend retreat of British Prime Ministers. In 1774, after nine years' service, its voters deprived Burke of his seat. Another was duly found for him at Molton, in Yorkshire, but before he could take up his duties he got a better, indeed, irresistible offer from Bristol, the second largest British city. He was to represent the place for six years (ibid.: 20).

Burke and Empire:
The Centre of His Life and Work

Barkan, exhibiting no sense of American hostility to empire as a political form, lays particular stress on the *imperial* dimension in Burke's thinking (Barkan 1972: xxiii). He applauds Burke's celebration of justice. Burke repudiated injustice – the misuse of rights and powers – everywhere in the British realm (Burke 1972: 11). This was as true at home as abroad, as true in Ireland and India, as crucial in North America, as it was anywhere in England.

The fate of the British Empire is the constant in Burke's preoccupations intellectually and politically. Three of his great concerns – Ireland, America and India – involved relations *within* the British territories. The fourth – France – involved the relations between the British and another great and rival empire, one which his greatest and most famous book identified as having gone catastrophically astray (Mitchell 1993: vii–xix). Though he wrote brilliantly on all of these relationships, he was not equally equipped in their regard in terms of experience. This point demands a few words.

Knowledge with and without Experience: The Status of Burke's Opinions

Burke is, necessarily, on surest ground speaking of places of which he has intimate experience. Burke's opinions and writings on England and Ireland and Anglo-Irish relations drew on a very direct and extensive experience which could be harnessed to the unusual powers of analysis and synthesis he demonstrated whenever he was intellectually engaged. O'Brien says Burke is best of all writing on Ireland (O'Brien 1988: xxxviii). The point, however, is surely that Burke also speaks very cogently about places he knows only by report. Wisdom evidently puts a premium on study. Indeed, if ever a man demonstrated that learning is ultimately more important than travel or foreign residence in international affairs, Burke was that man. He developed an expert knowledge of India and of the English American Colonies, though he had visited neither. He also wrote the most famous book ever on the French Revolution, though his spoken French was weak – indeed a source of embarrassment to him – and he had never spent any long periods in France. Even such time as he did spend in France was not in the Parisian metropolis but in provincial Auxerre. As L.G. Mitchell observes, while Fox, Rockingham and Grey spoke to Mirabeau, Talleyrand and La Fayette in Paris, Burke listened to the views of provincials barely known to history (Mitchell 1993: vi). Let us ponder a while the main geographical settings of his interests.

Burke on Ireland and the English/British Connection

Burke must have experienced a number of unresolved tensions in his combined role as critic and peacemaker. It is hardly surprising that he is in some respects something of a paradox, in terms of his religious and national identity alike. These two dimensions are, moreover, inevitably difficult at times to prise apart. Burke knew well how to oppose – and could be very touchy as Hill points out (Hill 1975: 44) – but he was also a reconciler of men and a healer of divisions. Himself a practicing Anglican, though soaked in Catholicism, he brought together in his person the two faiths which have principally divided the English since the Reformation and continue to divide their globally scattered descendants. This broad sense of Christianity and his manifest comfort with both persuasions he maintained his entire adult life. 'I am attached to Christianity at large' he declared (McCue 1997: 13). Clearly this mattered hugely to him with regard to Anglo-Irish relations.

There is no reason to doubt the sincerity of his profession of faith. It is very tempting, of course, to see Burke, as his enemies always did, as a concealed case of the cradle Catholic. He clearly felt a searing anger at the ill-treatment of Irish Catholicism. There is no mistaking the resentment in a letter he sent to his son Richard, with regard to the Oath of Conformity required of Catholics who wished to enter the professions:

> Let three millions of people but abandon all that they and their ancestors have been taught to believe sacred, and to foreswear it publicly in terms the most degrading, scurrilous, and indecent for men of integrity and virtue, and to abuse the whole of their former lives, and to slander the education they have received, – and nothing more is required of them. (O'Brien 1988: xxx)

We note again that Burke was at times 'prickly', especially with aristocratic mediocrities who had ready access to places he needed his special genius to reach (Hill 1975: 44). Burke seems nevertheless to have been endowed with the great Christian gift of loving pardon and forgiveness. Nor was this religious tolerance the end of his irenic gifts. Burke was also manifestly a man of two countries. Born and raised in Ireland, he spent most of his adult life in England, maintaining throughout his life a profound love of both countries.

O'Brien writes naturally enough of these never fully resolved tensions in Burke's mind, of his admiration for the achievements of the English/British and his intransigent hostility to the wrongs of the British and Protestant ascendancy in Ireland (O'Brien 1988: vii–xv). Such contradictions are not surprising. Even a mind as powerful as Burke's does not turn on logic and reason alone. Men absorb in the experience of life powerful affective loyalties to institutions and places, feelings which are not reducible to strict reasoning. Life is like art, being tolerant of ambiguity. The ambiguities of a mixed national or religious formation in an individual, lead, unsurprisingly, to powerful ambivalences both in that individual's outlook and inner life. This kind of psychological fracture is apparent in many writers born in one place and culture and living and flourishing in another place and culture, with their loyalties at once extended to both and yet somewhat torn between them. Kipling is surely another comparable case, a British imperialist born in India who admires the Empire and hates racial bigotry.

Burke, England and Ireland, Some Further Considerations

Burke never flinched throughout his life from spelling out English wrongs in Ireland. The very structure of the situation in Ireland was unjust, with the Catholic religion curtailed, and – as we now see clearly – a mainly Protestant landlord class ill-treating the peasantry.[7] Conor Cruise O'Brien writes tellingly of the tension, never fully resolved, between Burke's deep love of England and his enduring love, part conjoined with his care for England and part framed in opposition to British policy, for his native land.

Burke always opposed the persecution and marginalization of Catholicism in Ireland. In the first half of the 1760s, he opposed the 'Popery Laws' that kept Catholics out of the professions. There were also laws preventing primogeniture and enforcing coheir division among all male heirs and the same process on these heirs themselves at their deaths. As Burke plainly stated, this legislation was aimed at preventing long-term material prosperity and expansion of Catholic estates. Worse still, if a Catholic's eldest son conformed to the Church of Ireland he got control over his father's estate within the latter's lifetime. Similar rights were extended to other sons. Nor did these boys have to attain their majority for this change in their father's financial status. Children of immature years were eligible (Burke in O'Brien 1988: vii–xv).

Burke opposed the Protestant ascendancy in which the Catholic majority were held down by the Protestant Irish. Cumulatively, his attacks on the religious and economic persecution of Irish Catholics and his demand that Ireland be given the rights of free trade and released from the mercantilist restrictions placed on Irish economic life by British law, were probably to play a part in the eventual loss of his seat at Bristol (O'Brien 1997: 35–6).

One would like to report that Burke believed that the system of proprietorship and tenancy in Ireland was deeply flawed, cast indefensibly in the interests of the landlords. I have found no evidence that this was very central to his complaints. Overall, he understood perfectly the sources therefore of Irish nationalism, but feared, rightly, that given the configuration of political events in the late eighteenth century, it would be contaminated fatally by Jacobinism. And it is true that at times Irish rebels did reach out to French revolutionary or imperial republicanism. Some forty years after Burke had written on the Popery Laws, the Irish rebel, Robert Emmet, executed for treason in 1803, denied any treachery. In the middle of a vast European-wide conflict, however, Emmet had sought help for Irish independence with Bonaparte and Talleyrand. Burke, recently dead, was not there to comment. What might he have said? We may reasonably guess that he would have inquired as to what Ireland could have gained from such cynics, whose political and military expansion had already crushed many millions of people all over

Europe. A brave and fine speech in the face of British injustice does not betoken wise Irish policy.[8]

Burke and Relations with the North American Settlements

Burke's concern over Anglo-American relations was, consistently, the preservation of empire. His specific concern in 1765, says Elliott Barkan, had been the Repeal of the Stamp Act, a repeal he thought crucial to the preservation of *liberty* in the Empire (Barkan 1972: xi). He thought Parliament had the right of taxation but had exercised it in America unwisely and to British disadvantage (Burke 1972*b*: 11). Burke always saw taxation of the colonists as counterproductive, as his direct words to the House of Commons show:

> As you, however, still keep up the duty on tea, in order to preserve the right of taxation, they forbid the introduction of tea, in order to deny that right. (Burke 1972*b*: 23)[9]

The Currency and Stamp Acts threatened to paralyse the Colonial economy (ibid.: 11). Burke held, however, that if power was misused, the flaw was not in the structure of the situation but in the persons of the ministry. At the same time he rejected the American claim that either their charters or lack of representation exempted them from taxes. The 'No Taxation without Representation' refrain would apply to most English towns (ibid.: 11). Burke was ever the realist. After the Boston Tea Party in 1773, he urged the Repeal of the duty. Again in March 1775 he spoke in the Commons for three hours, advancing thirteen resolutions for conciliation. All was to no avail (ibid.: 70).

In this effort to defuse the crisis, Burke stressed the size of the American population, its wealth, the vastness of the City of Philadelphia, the second largest in the Empire. Commerce with the American colonies was of great importance to the British economy. But given the British political ideas which prevailed there, military force would never be an appropriate solution to colonial problems. The colonists had English ideas of liberty (Hill 1975: 24–5). To those souls who said that in the end the Americans must obey, Burke effectively replied that there is no one definition of political obligation (ibid.: 26). After the Declaration of Independence in 1776 Burke was notably at the forefront of those recognizing the reality of the situation. The American part of the Empire was irretrievably lost (ibid.: 25).

Barkan notes, rather drily, that Burke actually seemed not to have grasped that the Americans had transcended any secondary status politically and become a nation in their own right (Barkan 1972: xxvi).

Burke and India, the East India Company and Warren Hastings

Burke was recognized as a leading authority on India, despite lacking personal experience of the subcontinent. The broad history is well known. The informal control of the East India Company in the eighteenth century was a disgraceful story of pillage, at its most notorious under the tyrannical and corrupt rule of Warren Hastings, Governor General of Bengal (McCue 1997: 22). Consistent agitation against the Company and Warren Hastings, complaints whose best-known voice was Burke's, had the eventual effect of taming the company. Burke committed fifteen years to the matter, fired by profound indignation (ibid.: 21). In 1795 the acquittal of Hastings was a great blow to Burke (Burke in O'Brien 1997: 331), though the long-term effect of bringing the rule of law to imperial administration surely outweighed the shame of such a decision. In the nineteenth century India came under the British rule of law; arguably this was an advance whose beneficial influence persists to this day in India.

Hill stresses the admirable caution and probity with which Burke proceeded. In order for the British Crown to be justified in assuming political power in India, Burke maintained, what

was being abused by the East India Company – that is India
herself – must be great and important; the abuse too must
be great, habitual and incurable under present circumstances
(Hill 1975: 31). Burke maintained that India was the most
substantial part of the Empire following the loss of America,
and the rights and interests of the peoples of India had been
shamefully trampled on (ibid.: 28–31). Again this theme of the
dignity and importance of oppressed peoples came to the fore
in Burke's mind (ibid.: 31). He did not lightly contemplate
the overthrow of current British arrangements in India, but felt
obliged to recommend such in view of the incorrigible corruption involved.

Though Burke 'lost' the legal case against Warren Hastings,
the impeachment failing, the moral victory was surely his.
A more remarkable story still, however, was to be witnessed in
Burke's extraordinary and initially isolated prescience in the
case of the Revolution in France. What was the moral – properly
speaking *immoral* – essence of the Revolution in France according to Burke? Precisely what was it about this cataclysm that so
affronted him?

The Jacobin Menace: Burke's Opposition to the Revolution in France

Burke correctly divined in the French Revolution, a world-
moving upheaval. Strangely his book was very ill received at first,
especially in respect of its factual errors. According to L.G.
Mitchell, it was initially almost universally mocked and reviled
(Mitchell 1993: vii–ix). What later came to be widely recognized
as one of the masterpieces in the history of political discussion
drew its appeal, despite the book's undeniable empirical shortcomings, from Burke's matchless detection of the Revolution's
implacable intentions and boundless appetite for upheaval,
murder and revenge.

Burke was not opposed to the Enlightenment as such. It was
the dismissal of the lessons of history and the grotesque progeny

which this neglect can spawn which appalled him. He characterized the menace in France in the very early period as a rupture
between liberty and justice, leaving neither of them safe (O'Brien
1997: 208–9). Burke disassociated himself above all from the
rootless rationalism typical of the French Enlightenment. His
words confront the French directly:

> . . . you chose to act as if you had never been moulded into
> civil Society, and had everything to begin anew. You began ill
> because you began by despising everything that belonged to
> you. (Burke 1993: 36)

He repudiated the repudiation of the past, a rejection of
earlier times which in the French case united thinkers as
different as Voltaire and Rousseau. Burke opposed all schemes
of fundamentalist reconstruction and the formulation of policy
on the basis of purely abstract reasoning. Voltaire and Rousseau,
for all their considerable differences, agreed at least that one
should start with a clean slate and an abstract set of principles
about humanity. That is to say, they agreed on the very thing
which Burke denies. Of his contempt for their consuming
vanity his *Letter to a Member of the National Assembly* leaves us in
no doubt (Burke in O'Brien 1997: 242–3). Their theoretical
reification, as we might term it today, aroused in Burke a deep
distrust. This suspicion was the core of his opposition to the
Revolution in France, as he preferred to call the French Revolution. Burke's prescience in respect of this political earthquake
seems uncanny. As Bredvold and Ross point out, he even antici-
pated that a military adventurer-dictator of the type Napoleon
proved to be could emerge (Bredvold and Ross 1970: 3).

Burke, Enlightenment and Revolution:
A Case of Mixed Feelings

Given the breadth of his knowledge and interests, which
rival those of Sam Johnson, Burke appears as something of a

Renaissance man, an *uomo universale*. This is not something which in itself makes him especially opposed to the Enlightenment. It does not even imply that he did not subscribe to some of the prospectus. He was a close friend of Adam Smith, the greatest economist of the Enlightenment. The breadth of learning, however, does explain the roundedness of the man. If he laughed at certain aspects of Enlightenment vocabulary and pretensions, then it must be said that so did many French people (Martin 2001).

At the very beginning he had been merely cautious, and we might even say openminded about the Revolution, though he insisted that a people needs a degree of moderation in such dangerous circumstances. He moved very swiftly, however, into a more pessimistic mode (Burke in O'Brien 1997: 206-7). The monster was soon baring its teeth he believed, and the pillaging of church and aristocratic property was an attack upon all property (Burke in Mitchell 1993: xvii–xix).

Burke versus Constant on the Revolution

Benjamin Constant, some thirty-eight years younger than Burke, was better placed than he to assess the French upheaval. He was French-speaking and lived in Paris, where he observed things at first hand. From an initial sympathy, Constant soon moved to total opposition to the Revolution. He rightly characterized it as an *improbable* outcome of muddled thoughts on progress, coupled with a bad reading of history, specifically an ahistorical worship of the Greek city states (Constant 2003). Where he parted company with Burke was in his attitude to its future, a difference between the two men which exemplifies with startling clarity the difference between the liberal and the conservative. Constant, the liberal, cannot abandon his optimism. He thinks the Revolution is a one-off anomaly.[10]

The conservative Burke seems to have grasped the Revolution's insidious potential for mutation and reproduction in terms of a future template. He even, we have just noted, correctly predicted the possibility of its imminent transformation into military dictatorship. What with hindsight we can see, and what Constant shied away from, is that the Revolution in France was in the long run to prove a mere opening early shot, relatively restrained, in a new round of anomalous tyrannies. This was precisely the nightmare Burke feared. He would have been as horrified as Constant by the progeny of the Revolution in France, the political atavisms which a hundred and thirty years after Burke wrote were to sweep across almost half the globe, with the intention of taking *all* of it, in a total war against civilization both in its Christian and secular aspects. Unlike Constant, however, Burke would not have been surprised.

Burke's Views on Property

Burke held that the landed property of the aristocracy is the material base of civilization itself (Mitchell 1993: xvii–ix). Burke's approach to property is very sophisticated, as we shall see in a later chapter. For the present we can again make an illuminating comparison with Constant. Burke's preference for the property order is for the prevalence of *landed* wealth in the nation's property. A specific reason for his distrust of the French National Assembly was that it was not based on the landed interest (Hill 1975: 40). The new sources of bourgeois wealth, that is industrial and financial wealth, he distrusted, in France and England alike. He spoke of 'the warfare between the noble, ancient landed estate, and the new monied interest' (Burke 1770: 67). He should surely have deferred in this matter to his friend Adam Smith.

While Constant shares Burke's admiration for landed wealth, he takes a completely different view of the bourgeoisie and the middle classes which rise with the bourgeoisie (Constant 2003). Constant is surely right. In a few centuries the bourgeois order has done more for human economic welfare than millennia of

aristocratic dominance have achieved. And in any event the two
groups have now merged in the British case. The further twist in
the a priori rationalist nightmare, in which abstract and sentimental political schemes make war on property *in all its forms*
does not surface in Burke's writings. We may guess that in time
he would have come to approve and defend the bourgeois
order, with its extension and enlargement of the political
achievements of the landed interest.

Burke, Reform and Revolution

Burke was a conservative. He was not a reactionary nor an
opponent of reform. Indeed, Burke was a lifelong reformer
and exponent of a humane politics, as Bredvold and Ross point
out (Bredvold and Ross 1970: 2). He indeed engineered one
of the most important reforms of the eighteenth century, instantiated in his Bill for Economical Reform, often praised as the
most important single reform act of the eighteenth century in
England. It was pushed through against the opposition of
George III (McCue 1997: 27). He was a great publicist of the
American Revolution; he ceaselessly preached religious tolerance; he damned alike British corruption in India and the slave
trade (ibid.: 27). His support for the American colonists makes
clear that Burke does not oppose all revolutions. Elliott Barkan
points out that there is no contradiction, between Burke's
acceptance of and support for the American Revolution and
his hostility to the equally momentous Revolution in France.
This distinction involved no hypocrisy, merely a logical extension of his views on the dramatically contrasting nature of these
events (Barkan 1972: vii).

Burke's Critics and His Enthusiasts

Burke has enthusiastic defenders and critics. One can to some
degree discount indifference or invective in respect of Burke

when we find that men of the stature of Lord Macaulay so readily praise him. Macaulay speaks admiringly of Burke's 'comprehensive intellect'. He thought him the greatest Englishman
since Milton. On the very same page Macaulay homes in on one
of Burke's central constitutional principles. Burke, he observes,
held that the House of Commons is a check not on the people
but *for* the people (Macaulay 2008: 488).

Yet, well-known writers surprise us. Simon Schama in his huge
study of the French Revolution makes short shrift of Burke's
enormous contribution to the international understanding of
this world-changing upheaval. He is treated like an irrelevance
really (Schama 1990). Quite what Schama intends by this down-
playing is not easy to say. It is a bit akin to a study of the Greek
philosophers with no discussion of Plato.

A.J.P. Taylor's dismissal of Burke as 'a corrupt Whig Hack', is
as wrong as it is rude (Taylor 1976: 18). The intention behind
this abuse is less important than its probable provenance. It may
have been lifted from Marx. Marx too makes sneering remarks
about the 'bourgeois' Burke in *Capital*, 'that famous sophist and
sycophant' (Marx 1976: 440). That other less grand materialist,
Lewis Namier, who reduced everything to institutional interests,
also disliked Burke (O'Brien 1988: xx) though he did not like
Marx either, as he told Isaiah Berlin (Berlin 1980: 64–5).

Burke and the De-sanctification of Humanity

We live today, as Burke foresaw that future generations of
English-speakers would, in a society where the civilizing constraints of sanctity – piety, church-going, respect for religion and
other traditions – have been progressively dismantled. What
Burke called 'factious and seditious views' are widely taught in
our schools and universities. L.G. Mitchell draws attention to
Burke's understanding of the factional shape of politics in
late-eighteenth-century France, a factionalism which in Burke's
day was manifestly present in England (Mitchell 1993: x–xiii).

O'Brien notes that Burke's target is the English Jacobin faction, just as Orwell's in *Nineteen Eighty-Four* was the British Stalinist faction of the 1940s (O'Brien 1988: vii). Today, we need a new Burke to rebuke and expose these nihilists.

Particularly shocking is the pantheism and deification of the natural world which accompanies human spiritual de-sanctification. Chesterton was not as great an intellect as Burke, nor did he regard himself as a conservative; yet it is hard to imagine Burke's disagreeing with Chesterton, that credulity and superstition sat at the centre of intellectual life in the early twentieth century. Moreover, has not credulity swollen to baroque proportions in the subsequent hundred years? (McNamara and O'Keeffe 1988). That Burke predicted an era of madness is not the least of his many achievements. In subsequent chapters we will try to enlarge on the main features which have dominated this opening chapter.

2

Genial Olympian: Burke and His Opinions*

Introduction

Our first chapter sought to make it clear that Burke retained, throughout his lifetime, a wide range of political, social and – broadly speaking – philosophical interests of a conservative kind. He was not a very successful career politician. Indeed, he held ministerial office only briefly. That he was so influential, so commanding a figure, despite his relative failure in political preferment, speaks wonders for his powers of persuasion as writer, orator and political activist. His success was all the more extraordinary in that he was to some degree an outsider, an Irishman, enthusing over and exploring the complex political dynamics of a society that was his only by adoption, if we speak frankly.

In this chapter, we must above all interrogate Burke's lifelong criticism of the intellectual and political movement often known, in its day, and almost universally since, as the 'Enlightenment', the attempt, mainly under French guidance at first, to enlarge the secular claims of humanity, with regard to the world in which we live, and to deflate and demote the claims of religion in this regard. Our discussion will encounter certain ambiguities here. Though profoundly conservative in religion and politics alike, Burke was also a dedicated political reformer, even sometimes countenancing revolutions.

Given the rich variety of Burke's thinking, it will be useful to the reader if, initially, we spell out much more fully than was done in Chapter 1, Burke's main political opinions and preoccupations. Let us look in summary form at what Burke supports and rejects and then proceed to consider these two opposing categories at length, across his academic output as a whole.

This chapter must thus pay equal attention to what Burke applauded and what he opposed. One crucial issue is Burke's understanding of, and admiration for, the political institutions and practices of his adopted country. We will begin, then, with an account of what he favoured.

Political Themes and Contentions: What Burke Favoured

Burke greatly admired the general political conventions of England. It is a grave understatement to say that Burke admired English civilization. In truth England had him enthralled. First and foremost Burke admired the English constitution, which does not refer in the English/British case to a single document or even series of documents, but to the overall arrangements of political life.

What Burke most admired in his adopted country, was its ability to preserve its identity – its constitutional arrangements – over time, indeed its willingness to engage in *change* if necessary for this purpose. He believed that 'a state without the means of some change is without the means of its conservation' (Burke 1993: 21). This view is at the centre of Burke's politics. At root Burke was a staunch conservative, but a flexible one. He admired, from his eighteenth-century viewpoint, the arrangements in England in the last decade of the seventeenth century, whereby the safety of the realm was, in his view, saved from the dangers which had tragically and painfully disrupted it from the 1630s until the late 1680s. A few sketches of the period may serve the reader's understanding in some cases.

From the middle of the reign of Charles I (1625–49), England's governance had passed through great dangers. His years on the throne were confused and turbulent, with no settled consensus as to where power, authority and responsibility lay.[1] The country endured bitter civil war, the fearful event of Charles's execution in 1649, and even a brief period of republicanism under the Cromwells, father and son. The distribution of power between aristocracy, monarchy and Commons (the lower House of Parliament) had been disrupted, first with the monarchy seeking an absolute domination over the aristocracy and the Commons, and second with the attempt by the Commons, initially to subdue the aristocracy and contain the King, but subsequently to eliminate the monarchy in favour of a republic. Nor did the nation achieve a proper equilibrium after 1660, under the restored monarchy in the hectic reign of Charles II (1660–85). The short reign of Charles's younger brother James II (1685–88) had been even more troublesome; there was during his years on the throne an obvious desire by the royal family to revert to Catholicism.

Burke regarded these travails with horror. He saw as exemplary the English political and constitutional Settlement of 1689–1701, with its artfully reconstituted distribution of powers between Commons, nobility and monarchy. It had put the aristocracy back in charge, but not with absolute powers. The Settlement had brought the Protestant Dutch prince, William of Orange, to the throne (1689–1702), ruling jointly as William III with his wife Mary (1689-94) in a period crucial in the redefinition of the English polity after half a century of turmoil. Burke set his star across his entire adult life by the success of this reordering. He particularly favoured the aristocratic ascendancy, which the nobility, itself reconstituted, had engineered.

The Aristocratic Mode of Governance

The re-establishment of the aristocracy from 1689 meant a constitutional system that we may refer to as the 'Aristocratic Mode of Governance', in which a settled internal distribution of power was achieved between nobles, monarchy and Commons. All three sides of the triangle of power kept watch on one another, with the aristocracy generally dominant. Since the fifteenth century, however, ultimate financial control had rested with the Commons, a condition clearly involving some constraint on purely aristocratic power, one of which Burke very much approved (Burke 1975: 254–8).[2] Burke favoured aristocratic pre-eminence but not in an unlimited form. For Burke properly constituted politics is always subject to limits. Benjamin Constant, in some ways, as we suggested in Chapter 1, the slightly later French equivalent of a Burke, was, like Burke, impressed with the stability which the Whig oligarchy and a redefined monarchy had together brought to English politics: 'Heredity in England does not confer on its members a contested power, arbitrary and vexatious, but a specified authority and constitutional functions' (Constant 2003: 187).

Burke Also Admired the Way the English Aristocracy Recruited from Below

Under the 'aristocratic mode of governance', the distribution of power rested principally with the aristocracy, but in the context of mutual consent and a strong sense of duty among the powerful classes. Above all, heredity could be acquired. The aristocracy and its mode of governance were in England open to recruitment of talented persons from below. And Burke thoroughly approved. As he put it to the young French friend, whose letter of inquiry as to Burke's opinions on French events was the signal for Burke's most famous book:

> You do not imagine, that I wish to confine power, authority, and distinction to blood, and names, and titles. No, Sir. There is no qualification for government, but virtue and wisdom, actual or presumptive. Wherever they are actually found, they have, in whatever state, condition, profession or trade, the passport of Heaven to human place and honour. Woe to the

country which would madly and impiously reject the service of the talents and virtues, civil, military, or religious, that are given to grace and to serve it; and would condemn to obscurity every thing formed to diffuse lustre and glory around a state. (Burke 1790: 31)

The late Peter (Lord) Bauer believed that by international standards this social receptiveness to the low-born was unusually true of the English nobility and that such openness stretched across many years, indeed across centuries. Bauer has great fun listing the seemingly endless numbers of business people and politicians who have risen in modern times from humble beginnings (Bauer 1997). In fact, however, there has not been a closed aristocracy in England 'since the early Middle Ages' (ibid: 17). The aristocratic oligarchy always consisted, as Burke knew, in a mix of the well-born and those able and ambitious upwardly mobile souls – 'upward mobility' being the sociological metaphor we have used since the twentieth century to explain this kind of social change – whose notable talents were their credentials of ascent.

This receptiveness of the aristocracy to talent and enterprise from below, makes it clear that Burke's sense of aristocracy is not limited to the idea of the *nobility*. Rather the idea of the nobility is subsumed in the wider and vaguer concept of aristocracy. And it is the House of Commons which represents most the national interest by representing aristocracy in the broader sense.

We know that the British house of commons, without shutting its doors to any merit in any class, is, by the sure operation of adequate causes, filled with every thing illustrious in rank, in descent, in hereditary and in acquired opulence, in cultivated talents, in military, civil, naval, and politic distinction, that the country can afford. (Burke 1790: 27)

B.W. Hill points out that Burke repudiated theories of 'balance' in the nation's constitutional arrangements as 'hazardous'. While Burke yielded to no one in his admiration for the

constitutional settlement of the late seventeenth century, he saw
clearly that the historical tendency of British politics was to
elevate the importance of the Commons. The Commons were
the people's 'sole representatives' and the 'natural guardians of
the Constitution' (Burke 1975: 248–9).

We saw in Chapter 1 that Burke was occasionally peeved by
aristocratic nonentities who had effortless access to the high
places it took all his personal brilliance to reach; this in no way
detracted from his belief that the aristocracy as he understood
the term, had the ability and duty to supply a benign and patriotic form of political life to the society over whose management
it presided. To the extent that Burke was an important influence
in England his own story is a cogent example of the prudent
openness for which he praised the English nobles. Not only did
Burke hold that our aristocracy was well endowed with the
virtues required for the governance of Britain, but he also
thought it qualified for an international and imperial role.
We need therefore a few words on another of Burke's central
concerns: his understanding of the British Empire.

Burke as an Empire Enthusiast

Burke much admired the achievements of the overseas British
in America, India and elsewhere. Moreover, with Burke, support
for the Empire was a lifelong theme. From his earliest
times in Parliament, he was active in its cause. Unlike the English
monarchy, however, the British Empire did not have an ancient
history, and it was to last no more than a century and a half
after Burke's passing. It had been facilitated as an English, rather
than British venture, initially, by the opening up by European
peoples of the trans-oceanic trade routes from the fifteenth
century onwards. Our imperial beginnings lie mostly in the
seventeenth century. Today the British Empire has virtually ceased
to exist. Its high points were the eighteenth and nineteenth
centuries. In the nineteenth century it was the largest empire
the world has ever known.

Empires may be good or bad. Burke was a passionate believer in the British Empire and nation. He would certainly have known that many of the empires in history have been horrible, a consideration that applied to some in his day, and has often applied since. It would be very reasonable to propose that he would have been horrified at the reflex hostility that the ideas of a British nation and empire have aroused in British bien pensant intellectual life in the last 150 years. For much of the twentieth century the British Empire, its course nearly run, was excoriated in British universities and schools, as an engine of exploitation of colonial peoples. It was widely believed that the British had grown fat on such exploitation. It is only proper to point out that when Burke got involved in Indian affairs, it was to *prevent corruption and exploitation.*

It has not been sufficiently observed that Burke loved one empire and two nations. His support of empire as a political form had nothing of the universal in it. Rather it stemmed from his conviction that the British Empire was generally a benign force in the world. There are very many modern historians who would largely agree with this assessment. Niall Ferguson is one example (Ferguson 2003), Andrew Roberts another (Roberts 2006). There have at times been terrible crimes in British Imperial administration. It is really the balance of good and ill which has to be decided.

Hostility to imperialism, even to any hint of imperialism, is standard among many European intellectuals and also among non-European politicians. Whether the whole critique is quite so popular among the ordinary peoples whom the latter often so spectacularly exploit and neglect is more doubtful. In any case, European critics appeared quite early. Adam Smith is famous for having said empire was a waste of money (Smith 1976: 130–1). Frédéric Bastiat, another economist, was in the 1830s and 1840s the most prominent French critic (Bastiat 1995).[3] In Smith and Bastiat we perhaps hear the prosaic voice of economic accountancy. What Niall Ferguson makes clear is that whatever ills were involved, and he thinks there were many, economic modernity could not have been effected without a mediating imperial structure. His very scholarly and yet readable book is worthy of study for students of political science.

Ferguson says Burke shared the then standard belief that the British Empire differed from others in the degree of freedom it afforded people. 'Without freedom', Burke said in 1766, 'it would not be the British Empire' (Ferguson 2003: 54). Burke leaves us in no doubt as to his enthusiasm and pride:

> The Parliament of Great Britain sits at the head of her great empire in two capacities. One as the local legislature of this island. . . . The other . . . is what I call her *imperial character*, in which . . . she superintends all the several and inferior legislatures, and guides and controls them all, without annihilating any. (Burke 1975: 152)

In his *Speech in Opening the Impeachment of Warren Hastings*, Burke's underlying contention, according to B.W. Hill, is that 'a distant empire brought responsibilities as well as advantages to its rulers' (ibid.: 210).

Burke also advisedly maintained that aristocracy was a suitable arrangement for British possessions overseas, notably in the case of the colonies in North America, of whose achievements he was a frank admirer. Thus for Burke empire and aristocracy were dovetailing issues. In any case, in Burke's day, the critique of empire as an organizational form, in particular the viewpoint that is hostile to empire *tout court*, was not widely known. In any event, British activity in distant places had met Burke's first criterion of acceptance: it had proved itself.

Burke as a Conservative Reformer

Peter Stanlis has argued that Burke regarded a mix of prudence and expediency as crucial ingredients of political management (Stanlis 1958: 120). Since the vicissitudes of politics endlessly throw up imperatives for the reform or elimination of abuses, we are not surprised to observe in Burke a lifetime of devotion to policies for improvement and an oft demonstrated opposition to pig-headed commitment to indefensible practices. Burke's conservatism must never be taken as opposition to policies of reform. Within the context of his patriotic conservatism, his faith in the wisdom of the past and the way it lives in what we inherit from it, Burke was a great reformer. No one had a keener eye for abuses. He had all his life opposed, for example, what he saw as political and religious wrongdoing by the English Protestant ascendancy in Ireland (Burke 1988).[4] We argued in Chapter 1 that he pursued the essence of what he believed to be good conservatism, that is to say that he recognized necessary changes.

T.W. Copeland has drawn attention to the scope and lifelong duration of Burke's reforming work. In the early 1780s he had pushed through his Bill for Economical Reform, against the strong opposition of George III and his clique, perhaps the most important reform measure of the century (Copeland in McCue 1997). According to Bredvold and Ross the essence of this measure was its aim of correcting the wasteful organization of the royal establishment and even more the antiquated practices of royal patronage damaging to the integrity of the Commons (Bredvold and Ross 1970: 169). As was noted earlier, Burke was hostile neither to royalty nor aristocracy nor commons; indeed he favoured all three parts as coming together in a pattern of complement and opposition. He was well aware that a free and respectable government requires vigilant observation of its parts in relation to each other to inhibit any arbitrary tendencies in organization.

Copeland draws attention also to the struggle Burke waged in the late 1780s against the misgovernment of India. He was firmly against the slave trade, against the oppression of Catholics and dissenters, against the imprisonment of debtors (Copeland in McCue 1997: 28). It is proper to draw attention to the many things Burke opposed. It should be noted that Burke was opposed to trade restrictions and outraged that Ireland was not extended the courtesy of trading rights such as were freely bestowed on the American colonists. He spoke in the Commons in April and May 1778 in favour of the freeing up of Irish trade, of admitting 'the Irish nation to the privileges of British citizens' (O'Brien 1997: 93).

Burke attacked some policies because he wanted them reformed, because practically they sullied policies he favoured. Others he opposed because on intellectual principle they *threatened* the conservative political order he espoused. These latter considerations were the main substance of Burke's last and most famous book *Reflections on the Revolution in France* (Burke 1790).

Interestingly, however, his first book, *A Vindication of Natural Society* 1756, was also an attack of this kind. When we discuss Burke's intellectual output chronologically, it will prove very useful to find it bracketed at the start and the end by substantively very close theses, with political and moral thinking about what he opposed on conservative principle, as opposed to the many contingent abuses he saw as compromising arrangements he positively favoured. This last distinction needs some enlargement.

Sound Enterprise and Bad Practice: The End/Means Distinction in Burke

Since Burke's writings are mostly political, they contain much criticism, it being hard to conceive of political commentary in which critical assessments play no part. Burke's criticisms are made both against wrong conceptions and wrong practices. The former are criticisms at the level of ends, which is to say of larger human purposes. Criticisms of practices are simply criticisms at the level of means.

In most of his writing, when Burke inveighs against wrongdoing, he is opposing wrong administrative means being employed where the context of the enterprise is legitimate. The means involved may be very bad ones. For example, the Protestant ascendancy in Catholic Ireland is very bad. For Burke, however, the enterprise of English rule in Ireland is not wrong, not a wrong end. It is legitimate for ultimate power in Ireland to rest with the English Crown, acting through its Parliament in

London. It is not easy to legitimate English rule in Ireland, however, because of the indefensible discrimination against Catholics. Politics in Ireland is mediated, indefensibly, via a Protestant faction. This is an example of a legitimate enterprise, or end, being invalidated by wrong methods of application, by means which do not chime with the end pursued. Likewise, the enterprise involved in the British rule in India is not wrong. It is not even wrong for the Empire in India to be represented, in embryo at least, by the East India Company. At first Burke had supported the East India Company against the advances of Westminster. Some years later he came to change his mind and to regard the principles of sound political management in India as now infracted by the activities of the East India Company, under what he now saw as the insufferable leadership of Warren Hastings (O'Brien 1997).

In the case of the Revolution in France, not only are virtually all the rules of conduct under heinous principles but the enterprise itself is sick. To seek to replace and then recast anew, the order of politics in France, is for Burke an anomalous, immoral, reckless and indefensible exercise, intrinsically likely to engender the plot he so perceptively foresaw, to murder the Royalty and nobility and pillage the church. The whole derangement is also manifestly for export. There were eccentric clergymen and others in England willing to apply the same principles (Burke 1790).[5] Before we pursue these questions, some readers might find it useful if we looked in summary form at some of the writers who supplied Burke with particularly obvious targets.

Voltaire, Rousseau, Condorcet: Three Voices of the French Enlightenment

Voltaire (1694–1778), whose real name was François-Marie de Arouet, was a very gifted journalist, novelist and playwright with a vast knowledge of philosophy, though he was not a great philosopher. From our point of view he is notable for his brilliant leadership of the burgeoning anti-Christian stage of the French Enlightenment in the 1750s. This made him a target for Burke's youthful wrath in *A Vindication of Natural Society*, despite Voltaire's manifest admiration for British civilization.

Rousseau (1712–78), whose Christian names were Jean-Jacques, was a man of wide talents, intellectual and cultural. He is not regarded as a great philosopher, but he had enormous influence in his own day and subsequently. His theory of the general will, which is the fundamental prop of governance, to which in his view all people in society consent, even if they do not realize it, has been alleged to point the way both to Marxist Communism and to Nazism, whose elites similarly claimed to be fulfilling the whole public interest. The grounds for alleging that he is the principal inspirer of modern 'progressive' education theory and practice, moreover, are so strong as to be virtually unchallengeable. In overall terms, Rousseau is arguably the most influential thinker of the last few centuries. He attracted Burke's wrath in the latter's mature years, alike for his theories of governance and for what Burke saw as his odious moral character.

Condorcet (1743–94), whose real name was Marie-Jean-Antoine-Nicolas de Caritat, was a brilliantly gifted mathematician and philosopher of science who had a great impact on the intellectual movement which became known as 'positivism', the – broadly speaking – correct belief that science can teach us a lot, in neutral and objective terms, about the world, including the human world. He may properly be criticized, however, along with the French Enlightenment generally, for *overstating* the case for the scientific study of *humankind*, that is to say, for engaging in intellectual reductionism, in illegitimate simplification of the complex human reality and mystery.

From the Men to the Project and from the Project to Its Politics

What Burke held to be true of these men, holds almost by definition for the intellectual project of the French Enlightenment itself. Though there were good men in the French

Enlightenment, it is not greatly unfair to say that the French Revolution was fundamentally the politics of the French Enlightenment in action. For Burke, insofar as the steering of this antinomian crusade is in the hands of a Voltaire or, worse still a Rousseau, vast dangers will be summoned up. There is a scathing sarcasm in respect of Voltaire's religious scepticism in *Reflections* (Burke 1790: 129) and a blistering commentary on Rousseau's insufferable vanity in *A Letter to a Member of the National Assembly*, published, according to O'Brien, effectively as a postscript to *Reflections*, in January 1771. Burke here declares Rousseau as 'by his own account without a single virtue' (O'Brien 1997: 243). In the hands of such men the Enlightenment will be ungovernable in its hubris, will break all the bonds of caution which restrain a settled politics, and inflict vastly more hurts than benefits upon the people involved. In such circumstances the enterprise itself will be sick.

Burke's Religion: An Element of Dissembling?

Burke's thought has a religious basis. Canavan says of Burke that the notion of an intelligible and ordered universe is basic to all his thought.[6] He believes in divine providence; indeed Father Canavan says there was no Christian doctrine he believed in more profoundly (ibid.: 178). We are not left in the dark, either, as to his views on the anti-religionists. In *Reflections* he contrives to spear Rousseau, Voltaire and Helvetius all in one sentence:

> We are not the converts of Rousseau; we are not the disciples of Voltaire; Helvetius has made no progress amongst us. Atheists are not our preachers; madmen are not our lawgivers. (Burke 1790: 53)

Burke on Providence, Further Considered

Even as a young man Burke had profound religious faith. He kept a notebook with his distant cousin William Burke, during the 1750s (Burke 1957 in Canavan 1960: 30).[7] This obscure period in Burke's life, before he entered public affairs, was, as we saw in Chapter 1, sometimes thought to be a barren one. The *Notebook* is yet one more example of the reasons we should not accept any such view. One of the essays in the Notebook has no title, though a subsequent one, 'Religion' was allotted to it (ibid.: 30–3). In this essay it is alleged that humans, with the hopes and fears under which they live, should seek understanding of the moral life not in 'Metaphysical or Physical speculation' (not in abstract general reasoning or in reasoning about the material universe, since these lead to mechanistic and inexorable explanations of human circumstance) but in divine providence. A loving God could not provide *fatally* for all things. It is of the essence of a divinely created being that humans are free.

An un-free world would not be consistent with the passions (feelings) of love, fear and hope, which God has also placed in us. Reasonings, metaphysical or physical, may tend to deny divine providence and human freedom. Consideration of human passions (feelings) tends to uphold them. A very similar idea is behind the famous statement of Burke's friend, Dr Samuel Johnson: 'We know our will is free and there's an end on't'.

Enlightenment, Human Loss and Burke's Christianity

For souls like Burke, hope is a crucial accompaniment to the faith which is the central demand made on humans by Christianity, indeed, by all three of the Judaic religions. Burke's providentialism expresses the hope as well as the faithful belief that behind and beneath the ebb and flow of pain and heartache which so often define our human lot, God's loving grace ultimately sustains us. There is no ducking the ugly truth that some of the Enlightenment's effects converge in a frightening sense of loss.

It is probable, even so, despite his faith that Burke dissembled somewhat in matters of religion. We have noted his pity for the oppressed Catholics of Ireland. His anger and distress when he saw what the French revolutionaries were doing to the Catholic church in France are painfully visible in his writing (Burke 1790: 90). He certainly married a Catholic and visited France in the year he married. As O'Brien points out, on this issue of a possible Catholic marriage we do *not* know. No record has been found. O'Brien makes so bold as to say, however, that Jane Nugent, who practised the Catholic faith all her life, would have insisted on a Catholic marriage. Since this could not have taken place in England or Ireland, it may well have been a Catholic marriage in France (McCue 1997: 16). Sometimes, as O'Brien points out, Burke is forced into a politic silence. This was the case when the American colonial rebels experienced the 'anti-Catholic paroxysm' of 1774–75. This potentially fatal upsurge was corrected by Washington, with his need for allies and supporters. The point here is that while Burke courageously defended Catholics, he could not directly expose himself to the charge of pro-Catholicism (ibid.: 49–50).

Burke's self-confessed comfort with Christianity *generally* was, however, genuine enough. Some of Burke's praise of Protestantism sounds entirely genuine. There are in *Reflections* some very positive arguments for the superiority of the Protestant persuasion in Christianity:

> Violently condemning neither the Greek nor the Armenian, nor, since heats are subsided, the Roman system of religion, we prefer the Protestant; not because we think it has less of the Christian religion in it, but because, in our judgment, it has more. We are Protestants, not from indifference, but from zeal. (Burke 1790: 55)

It may be that the kind of ambiguities we spoke of in Chapter 1, uncertainties bound to attach to a life like Burke's, spanning as it did two historically often mutually hostile races and religious cultures, did indeed leave him with unresolved ambivalences and even the need to trim expeditiously from time to time. On the other hand Burke is able openly to show himself totally opposed to the plundering of the French Church by the Revolutionaries. It is true that his enemies and opponents alleged that he was a secret Catholic. It is also true that he often leaves us wondering on this score. Perhaps the best move in the face of these difficulties is to remember that Burke was a very public and prominent *Christian*.

Here, however, after this brief sketch of Burke's intellectual mindset, we must begin to peruse, wherever possible, sequentially, the books and writings themselves.

Age and Achievement: Burke's Writings in Chronological Order

A Vindication of Natural Society (1756)

As was noted in Chapter 1, Burke had written brilliantly about the perils of human pride and folly when he was only twenty-seven, in his satire of the Enlightenment, *A Vindication Of Natural Society*. We can fairly say, by comparing its subject matter to that of *Reflections*, that Burke's concerns with what he regarded as a dangerous thinking were among his *life-time* preoccupations. We can legitimately be thinking of both books when we consider the first. This early book, too, was concerned with abstract reasoning lacking any lodgement in historical reality. Both books are fundamentally criticisms of the French Enlightenment. Burke thought the new continental philosophy as dangerous to order as to morality.

The ostensible target of this first book was Henry St John, Viscount Bolingbroke, a deist, rationalist philosopher of the first half of the eighteenth century, whom Burke regarded as an antinomian. The real target, however, was probably Voltaire, as O'Brien points out in some very powerful pages, in which he also observes that Bolingbroke was Voltaire's leading

intellectual disciple in England (O'Brien 1997: 253–5). The
ostensible thesis of *Vindication* was that 'political society' had
led to endless murder and enslavement of the many by the
few and exposed men to the plots of a 'few mad, designing or
ambitious priests'. It was roundly proposed that all 'species of
government' were equally remiss and that all our woes flowed
from neglect of the gift of 'natural reason' with which Providence
had equipped us.

Vindication was not, initially, much of a success. The satire
somewhat misfired. It was perhaps too oblique. That clarity of
intention was not achieved is witnessed in Murray Rothbard's
having taken it for an anarchist tract (Rothbard 1958). Rothbard
denies that it is at all satirical or ironic. In the event, as Hill
says, the criticism of all religious and political institutions in the
pamphlet was so sharp that when its true authorship was known
the opprobrium was partly re-directed at Burke himself (Hill
1975: 12).

The title itself *is* ironic, since Burke rejected the eighteenth
century's tendency to oppose the 'natural' to the 'artificial'.
Burke believed that the argument for 'natural' religion, without
revelation, church or dogma, paved the way for 'natural' society,
that is, a society devoid of its institutions (Burke 1975: 253–4).
Rothbard's idiosyncratic interpretation probably reduces to
Burke's incapacity for ironic writing. Certainly everything else
Burke wrote or said seems to contradict Rothbard's intellectual
interpretation.

O'Brien lauds the young Burke's extraordinary perspicacity.
In *Vindication* Burke is describing the pre-revolutionary process,
then in an early state. From his profound ability to judge the
here and now, Burke proceeded to gauge its later consequences.
He saw that if Christian belief could be subverted, so could the
state. 'The engines employed for the destruction of religion' by
Voltaire and his clique could also be used, though this was not
Voltaire's intention, to subvert government (O'Brien 1997:
253–5). The *philosophes* did not know they were subverting the
state, but Burke did. And he wanted to warn against them.

Burke does not name Voltaire, indeed he is careful not to, because the latter was famous – or notorious – for attacking Roman Catholicism. Even so it is hard not to see Voltaire in the satire. Burke had excoriated Bolingbroke (Voltaire) for his ahistorical rationalism, his tendency to argue from first premises remote from present and historically rooted realities. Defending Catholicism frontally, however, was inexpedient for Burke, and would have damaged his credibility (ibid.: 255). This tacking is surely pardonable and compensated for by Burke's having 'denounced in embryo' the ideological phenomenon he was to fight in its mature form from 1790 to his death in 1797, forty-one years after the publication of his first book.

Thus Burke's publications begin with one book, and end, give or take some very interesting articles, with another, both devoted overwhelmingly to what Burke saw as the – predominantly French – dangers to European civilization. They had the same targets: vainglorious projects comprising vast, sentimental abstractions, abandoning sane and temperate political reason and historically rooted, and in Burke's view, divinely ordained practicalities. Burke's last major work, *Reflections* was published in 1790, when the author was sixty-one and had only six more years to live. By reason of their conceptual closeness, their intellectual concern with much the same subject matter, the two books make up a powerful thematic frame for the whole Burkean corpus.

A Philosophical Inquiry into the Origin of Our Ideas on the Sublime and the Beautiful (1757)

This, Burke's second book, was published a year after *Vindication* and in Chapter 1 I identified it as belonging to the genre of philosophical psychology. As a treatise on aesthetics, remarkably sophisticated in so young an author, it is not greatly significant in relation to the political questions which dominated Burke's thinking. Beauty, Burke says, for example, resides in objects, being the quality in bodies which causes love or like emotions, by 'acting mechanically on the mind by the intervention of the senses' (Burke 1803–27: 235). Our sense of the beautiful resembles our sense of the moral in that both are implanted by divine providence. The order of morality, too, is reached by natural sentiment, not by speculative reasoning, the 'languid and precarious operation of our reason' (Canavan 1960: 56). People can behave morally without ever intellectualizing their moral life. The principles of taste, however, while they are open to rational investigation are distinct from the principles of reason. Our moral nature, by contrast, is known and understood by reason's investigation of it in a way that our aesthetic life cannot be. Burke's central notion in morality and politics is *order*, as known by reason (ibid.: 40). Canavan says *The Sublime and the Beautiful* does conform to Burke's blanket contempt for abstracted reflection. Burke always prefers the rooted and concrete to the abstract. But it cannot be said to connect much with the mix of religious inspiration and empirically grounded reflection which guided Burke's political writings. The work therefore provides no guide to Burke's moral and political thought.

Review of Adam Smith's *Theory of the Moral Sentiments* in Burke's Journal *Annual Register*, II (1759)

That Burke believes that morality and propriety are founded in our human feelings is also made apparent in his review of his friend Adam Smith's book, *Theory of the Moral Sentiments*. Smith and Burke share the same approach to the origin of moral ideas. He describes the Smith text as 'just, and founded on truth and nature'. Smith, he says, 'seeks for the just, the fit, the proper and the decent, in our most common and allowed passions' (Burke 1759: 485). Burke and Smith deny the a priori rationalism of the European Enlightenment, certainly when it comes to morality, which they regard as implanted by divine providence

in human nature. This does not put them at odds with enlightenment as an idea. Smith is regarded, indeed, as the greatest
economist of the Enlightenment. Burke and the Enlightenment
is not a standard coupling of nouns. Even so, who is more
enlightened in the dictionary sense than a man who was palpa-
bly the enemy of human cruelty and rapacity in all its manifestations? To parody his friend Dr Johnson's words on Pope,
'if Burke be not enlightened, where is enlightenment to be
found?'[8]

Thoughts on the Present Discontents (1770)

This work has significance for much of modern British life.
It was written in response to the troubles of the 1760s, and its
principal aim was to clarify the policies of the Rockinghams.
The decade was marked by political disarray, with both parties
crushed and pressurized by George III's anti-parliamentary
politics and additionally riven by internal struggle. Burke strove
to insert a little coherence into proceedings by splicing a
Whig Fragment with a Tory one to form the New Whigs. He
particularly wanted to see more orderly conduct of political
business.

We will return briefly to the seminal ideas of this essay in
Chapter 3. Burke, ever the realist, is concerned with the
practicable:

> The question is not concerning absolute discontent or perfect
> satisfaction in Government, neither of which can be pure and
> unmixed at any time or upon any system. The controversy is
> about that degree of good-humour in the people, which may
> possibly be attained, and ought certainly to be looked for.
> (Burke 1770: 23).

In a very much later work, *Second Letter on a Regicide Peace*,
Burke pronounces formally on the practical rules of political
conduct. He claims that 'the rules of prudence . . . are formed

on the known march of the ordinary providence of God' (Burke 1796 in Canavan 1960: 14). There is, indeed, a certain flexibility in these prudential rules. Their application calls for a subtle intuitiveness. This does not make them valueless. As Burke says in *Present Discontents*:

> No lines can be laid down for civil or political wisdom. They are a matter incapable of exact definition. But, though no man can draw a stroke between the confines of day and night, yet light and darkness are upon the whole tolerably distinguishable. Nor will it be impossible for a Prince to find out such a mode of government, and such persons to administer it, as will give a great degree of content to his people, without any curious and anxious research for that abstract, universal, perfect harmony, which, while he is seeking, he abandons those means of ordinary tranquillity which are in his power without any research at all. (Burke 1770: 43)

This is Burke explaining in the simplest of language the Christian conception of the nature of our prudential moral life. It is utterly opposite from the sentimental abstract search for secular perfection. From this prudential reasoning all the civilized possibilities of law and politics proceed. A civilized politics requires that we know that the political good, though concrete, is also exceedingly complex and requires approximations on the part of political decision-makers, given the impossibility of perfection (Canavan 1960: 9–10).

'Speech to the Electors of Bristol' (November 1774)

This speech actually took place after one of the two speeches on America included in this chapter, the first of which in our selection, on American Taxation, was delivered in April of 1774. This slight deviation in terms of strict chronology is done for sensible analytical purposes. The two American speeches form a pair. In his 'Speech to the Electors of Bristol', delivered almost immediately after the election which made him Bristol's MP, Burke pronounced that Members of Parliament are not delegates, they are not members of the area which has voted them in, but members of Parliament (Burke 1975: 157–8). This is a profoundly important issue in the operation of politics. The speech is thus of great historical importance in respect of the functional aspects of the British constitution, in Burke's interpretations of members' duties:

> . . . *authoritative* instructions; *Mandates* issued, which the Member is bound blindly and implicitly to obey, to vote, and to argue for, though contrary to the clearest conviction of his judgement and conscience; these are things utterly unknown to the laws of this land, and which arise from a fundamental Mistake of the whole order and tenor of our Constitution. (ibid.: 157–8)

Burke insists that the representative duty of a Member of Parliament is to employ his knowledge and intellect to best purpose. He is not a supine delegate. Burke's political thinking and his political life too, however, were also guided by his religious beliefs. Much nearer to the close of his tenure of the Bristol seat, in 1780, as we shall see later, he was to write a letter (in 1777) to the Sheriffs of Bristol, outlining with surpassing clarity, his fundamental belief in political obligation, as defined by the ordinances of Revelation.

Burke on America: *Speech on American Taxation* (1774)

As Canavan points out, Burke's hostility to raising fundamental questions of society and politics was manifested in his refusal to talk about the sovereign rights of Parliament during the American crisis. The relationship between Parliament and the colonial legislatures had reconciled 'two very difficult points, superiority in the presiding state and freedom in the subordinate'. In the absence of unnecessary questioning this could continue to work (Burke 1769 in Canavan 1960: 68). Abstract political philosophy – such as questions about rights of sovereign and subject – should be left safely to the various schools of philosophy and politics.

Elliott Barkan relays the well-known view that the speech on American taxation is an example of superb rhetoric. One can search the text almost randomly for demonstration of this:

But if, intemperately, unwisely, fatally, you sophisticate and poison the very source of government, by urging subtle deductions, and consequences odious to those you govern, from the unlimited and illimitable nature of supreme sovereignty, you will teach them by these means to call that sovereignty itself in question. (Burke 1972*b*: 65)

Burke regarded obstinacy as a vice, a point he also made clear in this same speech. Obstinacy in favour of the indefensible was unsound conservative politics:

But among vices, there is none which the House abhors in the same degree with obstinacy. Obstinacy, sir, is certainly a great vice, and in the changeful state of political affairs it is frequently the cause of great mischief. (Ibid: 61)

Burke had long argued that the American colonists had become accustomed to liberty and that this was something British political management must respect. If the British government wished to reason rightly about the Americans, it must respect the idea that liberty is crucial to the political good and includes the right to self-taxation (Canavan 1960: 7–8).

Again, and again, revert to your own principles – *Seek Peace, and ensue it* – leave America, if she has taxable matter in her, to tax herself. I am not here going into the distinctions of rights, not attempting to mark their boundaries. I do not enter into these metaphysical distinctions; I hate the very sound of them. Leave the Americans as they antiently stood, and these distinctions, born of our unhappy contest, will die along with it. Be content to bind America by laws of trade. . . . Do not burthen them by taxes. . . . (Burke 1999: 78)

The spirit of prudent practicality – what Canavan calls Burke's 'practical reason' – here quite typically infuses Burke's words (Canavan 1960: 3–27). He thought of the shortcomings of British tax policy in the American colonies as constituting a failure to meet the required imperial standards. Unjust taxation like the Stamp Act was prejudicial to the cause of *liberty in the Empire*. At the early age of thirty-seven Burke was active in the repeal of this hated tax. His reputation as a speaker of note was formed in this experience (Hill 1975: 14).

It is important to understand what was involved. Burke believed that Parliament, which was 'the superintending legislature of the empire', as Elliott Barkan puts it, indisputably had the *right* to levy taxes in the overseas territories. The prudential side of his understanding, however, told him that the practice was not always helpful. Parliamentary supremacy was the key issue, everywhere in the imperial territories. If there were difficulties, these involved the political actors, not the political system based on the Settlement of 1689, which Burke so revered. It was a matter of upholding Parliamentary sovereignty judiciously. If power was misused, this was a fault of the specific administrators, in no way undermining the admiral caution and stabilizing constraints in the system itself. All rights and powers resided with Parliament. To surrender any of them would sully Parliament's authority and consequently threaten the solidarity of the Empire (Barkan 1972: xi–xii).

Speech in Support of Resolutions for Conciliation with the American Colonies (1775)

Here Burke points out to the Commons that 'the march of the human mind is slow'. It took two hundred years, after Wales had been annexed by the English Crown, for the recognition to dawn that oppressive political control is counterproductive in every way. Thus in the twenty-seventh year of the reign of Henry VIII, Wales was given all the rights granted to English subjects, and in the thirty-fifth year the grant of their own property, with the establishment of proper counties and boroughs (Burke 1972*a*: 100–1).

McCue says that in Burke's view Britain could and should govern the American colonies, and Ireland too, but only with the consent of the governed. Once consent is lost it is lost (McCue 1997). What seems surprising today is that Burke did not witness in the American upsurge the signs of a nascent new order of politics. Perhaps our minds may be simply overwhelmed by our factual knowledge (of what happened) and in a reflex sense indisposed to be influenced by the counterfactual (alternative) possibilities. For example, we should try to imagine the continuation of British hegemony in North America. American independence looks 'inevitable' to us, but is it outrageous to consider the possibility of a century or two more of British domination? To cite a somewhat parallel case, not long ago the Soviet Union looked like a permanent feature of the world.

Burke's *Letter to the Sheriffs of Bristol* (1776)

We turn now to the second famous Bristol text, the letter to the Sheriffs of Bristol. Readers will remember that we decided to keep two of the American texts together for conceptual clarity and impact, though this broke strict chronology of output. In the case of Burke's two well-known sets of remarks to Bristol audiences, we have kept them apart because they constitute a rough frame for his period as the Bristol MP, though the *Letter to the Sheriffs* actually precedes the loss of the seat by Burke in 1780.

The *Letter*'s principal practical emphasis is to the effect that when one community is subordinate to another the superior is often tempted to pride and self-complacency. The text makes clear that in Burke's view the war in America, 'the most impolitic we ever carried on', is a product of the country's rash forgetting of this danger (Burke 1975: 191). The letter has a profoundly philosophic quality along with its practical and prudential caution, and carries us to the heart of Burke's philosophy of politics. 'Liberty . . . must be limited in order to be possessed' (ibid.: 199).

Burke on India

Burke was the leading member of the Select Committee of the Commons set up in 1781 to examine the ineffective and anomalous rule of India by the East India Company. Burke had initially favoured its rule. Until 1773, he had opposed ministerial attempts to control it. By 1782 he had completely changed his mind, urging Parliamentary control. Burke was now anxious to right the wrongs India had endured under George III, and deeply angered by the evidence uncovered of corruption and tyranny under Warren Hastings, Governor General of Bengal, and determined to bring him to justice. The result was the India Bill of 1783, which transferred the government of India formally to the British Parliament. In the coming to fruition of this Bill, Burke's labours with regard to political decencies in India were crucial (O'Brien 1997: 163). His famous speech in favour of Fox's East India Bill epitomizes his contribution. It did not succeed, but it was part of a succession of measures which eventually did contrive to bring India under the control of the Westminster Parliament.

This was crucial. Whatever its beginnings the East India Company had in time become a monster. Were the whole history of the British Empire comparable, that history would not be the mostly benign and productive story it is often regarded as. The people of India, says Burke, are 'undone' (Burke 1975:

237). 'The Company has made a common cause and identified themselves with the destroyers of India' (ibid.: 236). Not only did Hastings and his Company ruthlessly exploit and crush the indigenous population; they also persecuted and even murdered Britons sent out to investigate the various atrocities:

> Thus the servants of the East India Company triumph, and the representatives of the people of Great Britain are defeated. I therefore conclude, what you all conclude, that this body, being totally perverted from the purposes of its institution, is utterly incorrigible; and because they are incorrigible, power should be taken out of their hands, just on the same principles on which have been made all the just changes and revolutions of government that have taken place since the beginning of the world. (Ibid: 236)

Speech on Fox's East India Bill (1783)

The actual author of this Bill, though it carries the name 'Fox', was Burke himself. Hill points out that the theme of the speech is a lifetime constant in Burke, namely the responsibility of government with respect to the governed (ibid.: 60). It was for its violation of the responsibilities of government that Burke eventually took sides against the East India Company and its Governor General, Warren Hastings. Though the attempted impeachment of the latter failed, the Bill and the Speech are widely credited with a major role in supplying India with proper governance.

Hill believes that the importance of the speech is not in the details of the allegations made, since Burke was so enraged at the time of writing as to be somewhat intemperate (Hill in Burke 1975: 210). What matters in the speech is Burke's insistence on the duties of government, its responsibilities. In the case of the East India Company, these obligations, according to Burke, have not been met. The Company does not look after its Indian charges as it should. Burke says:

> Magna Charta is a Charter to restrain power and to destroy monopoly. The East Indian Charter is a Charter to establish monopoly and to create power. (Burke 1975: 210)

Hill rightly says that when Burke goes on the attack, it is always to censure those who exceed the bounds of political morality (ibid.: 210–11). In this speech, Burke does indeed detail the corruption and cruelty of the East India Company. More important by far and something which Hill strangely ignores, however, is the insistence which the speech makes on *natural rights*. Indeed, the importance of this matter would be hard to overstate in a work seeking to uncover and explain Burke's fundamental beliefs. As we have already noted, and as we shall see again in Chapter 3, Burke has widely been taken as a Utilitarian, that is to say, as one who believes that the business of morality, namely the management of social life and political order, should be guided fundamentally by *utility*, that is to say, by what has been shown by experience to be useful, practical, acceptable and beneficial to most people. Burke has been said to have subscribed to Utilitarianism even by writers who generally applaud his political opinions and intellectual achievements. I repeat that we shall say something more about this in Chapter 3 but it does also call for further discussion now.

It is certainly not the case that Burke would do anything so silly as to reject utility, or in everyday language, *usefulness*, as an idea and principle. What he would reject is the claim that utility can constitute the deep core of morality. In other words, the useful is an important secondary moral category, arising from primary moral goods such as freedom and right action.[9] For Burke, the claim that the useful is paramount would amount to denying the existence of any moral order at all. What Burke objected to in moral and political life was the kind of shallow and sentimental thinking which characterized much of the

French Enlightenment. For Burke one does not talk about rights unless the matter is serious and the language adequate to the seriousness.

Loose and promiscuous attitudinizing, of a kind which brutally extinguishes the past and lays waste the future: such is Burke's fundamental assessment of the developments which he saw in France, developments already boasting converts in England, and which he feared might spread further in his adopted land. His two particular bêtes noires, if readers will forgive the French metaphor, were the prominent rightsologists – as we might call them today, Voltaire and Rousseau. He does not pursue them on grounds solely of practicality, but on grounds of fundamental principle also.

Rights exist and are of infinite importance to Burke, since he believes they come from God. In this speech Burke maintains, beyond all question of ambiguity, that '(t)he rights of *men* – that is to say the natural rights of mankind – are indeed sacred things; and if any public measure is proved mischievously to affect them, the objection ought to be fatal to that measure . . .'.

Burke's Irish Writings: *An Unfinished Letter to His Son* (179–)

Burke was during his lifetime a major influence on 'conservative' thought, those doctrines and theories attempting to build on the successful past history of polities and extend present successes into the future for generations to come. Burke's influence on conservative thinking has since been unquestionably enormous. Despite his undoubted love of his native land and what seem to me his unmistakable Catholic sympathies, however, his impact on Irish affairs was limited in scope. He wrote no books, though there are some fine letters and speeches, brought together first in a famous selection by Matthew Arnold. This was re-issued in 1988 with a new introduction by Conor Cruise O'Brien (Burke 1988).

Why though, is there no big Irish book by Burke? What part if any Burke's thinking may have played in the English-speaking world in general today, is a subject to be touched on in Chapter 4. To repeat: it cannot be claimed that his writings much influenced events in Ireland either in or after his lifetime. O'Brien believes that Burke felt guilty about how little overall he had done to relieve the oppression of the Irish. In India he had been much more successful at righting wrongs. His need to compound for Irish failure was transferred to the Indian question (Burke 1988: 336).

His Irish writings stretch across more than forty years. A fine, beautifully crafted example, though it was never finished, was his letter to his son, Richard, in the early 1790s. Including it here ostensibly offends our intended chronology since it was penned after *Reflections*. Breaking the order is once again excusable, however. Burke's writings on Ireland are continual and consistent across his lifetime. Moreover, Ireland did not undergo in the eighteenth century, or since, any convulsion like the Revolution in France, not only colossal in its national but also in its international implications. The horrors of the 1840s Irish famine were not even dreamed of in Burke's day and in any case, even had they occurred sixty years earlier, they were by comparison with the French upheaval an undeliberated and accidental calamity despite their frightful scale. Only one great climacteric in Burke's lifetime, what Burke saw as the impious Revolution in France, demanded the full angry force of his intellectual powers. We can properly say that *Reflections* was wrenched from his soul by the French cataclysm. There is simply no Irish counterpart.

A Letter to Richard Burke begins by identifying his son's task as an agent for the Catholics of Ireland, as comparable to his father's care. 'You are engaged in an undertaking similar in its principle to mine. You are engaged in the relief of an oppressed people' (ibid.: 343). Burke also says that the Protestant monopoly hurts the Protestants almost as much as the Catholics (ibid.: 345). The Protestant Ascendancy is the rule of a faction, who consider themselves 'sole citizens' (ibid.: 349). There can be no liberty in such circumstances, for how can liberty be 'made up of penalties . . . of incapacities'? (ibid.: 346).

The essay is a fine one. The condemnation is unanswerable. The explanation of such dreary despotism as it describes and condemns, however, is not the stuff of which great books are made. History is littered with factional political dispensations by definition incapable of a care for the general interest. Dull and corrupt forms of governance of this kind abound still in the poor world. They could hardly inspire a masterpiece on the lines of *Reflections*.

O'Brien says the tendency of Burke's writings on the Penal Laws was to arouse sympathy for the ruthlessly downtrodden Irish Catholic peasant-farmers, subjected as they were to a privileged, mainly Protestant landlord class (O'Brien 1988: xix). Seven decades later these agrarian wrongs were still unaddressed and attracting the attention of a great French liberal market theorist. In the 1840s, Frédéric Bastiat, in his 'Thoughts on Sharecropping', had pointed out that farm leases were extraordinarily short in Ireland, often for one year only. This was injustice institutionalized. If the tenant had a good crop a landlord might – and routinely did – pull him back immediately to his original financial position by raising the rental (Bastiat, forthcoming).

O'Brien points out that there was no significant move to redress these evils until after the Great Famine of the 1840s and the establishment of the Land League with its huge strengthening of the Irish tenant farmers (O'Brien 1988: ix–x). Burke had exposed the wrong in broad and general terms, a hundred and thirty years before history had moved to redress it (ibid.: xiii–xix). The exposure was in its way as great a triumph as Burke's correct characterization of the evils of the Revolution in France.

Reflections on the Revolution in France (1790), as a guide to Burke's oeuvre

Reflections, which was published in November 1790, is both the high point and effectively a kind of summary account of Burke's lifetime of political reasoning.[10] A key aim of this chapter is to convey to the reader some real sense of Burke's *magnum opus*. We will follow the standard convention of examining Burke's most famous work in more detail than in the case of his other writings. Success in this aim will permit *Reflections* to serve as a set of references for a broad evaluation. There is a strict limitation to this procedure, simply because many Burkean themes are not treated in *Reflections*. Even so, it may serve to shed a little light on the questions of substance, continuity and development in Burke's thinking.

Certainly, the consequences of the French upheaval as discerned by Burke, make up the most vital substance of this book. Some of these consequences he merely had to describe, which he did, very vividly. Others at the time of his writing had not yet taken material shape, though he foresaw them in outline and essence with extraordinary accuracy. We have already seen that Burke's critique of the 'Enlightenment' long pre-dated those actual years of the Revolution in France, during which the movement attained its disastrous initial momentum. The new French or French-inspired thinking had been the subject of his very first book. The gathering momentum of this thinking was to overthrow one of the world's most outstanding royal dynasties. At this point in our account, it might, perhaps for some of our readers, be helpful if we were to say a little in very brief compass about the course of the famous French Revolution, or as Burke preferred to call it, the Revolution in France.

The French Revolution: A Summary Account

The French Revolution, 1789–99 is often regarded as the key event in modern French history. It is not clear whether Burke was right that the cataclysm could have been avoided by the exercise of political wisdom and that from the ruins of monarchical absolutism a constitutional monarchy could have been raised. Edward Thomson says the greatest structural weakness in France was the insolvency of the monarchy (Thomson 1962: 5).

There were others. The aristocracy, the First Estate, was weak and unpopular. The Roman Catholic Church too, the Second Estate, was unpopular and intellectual life was infected with anticlericalism and an extreme ahistorical rationalism. This way of thinking came from the intellectuals of the Third Estate. The Third Estate also included the bourgeoisie and the lower orders, many of whom were restive. The businessmen looked for increased power and influence and the peasants and other countryfolk were burdened with heavy taxation. During the course of 1789 the power of the aristocracy and monarchy was broken and a National Assembly dominated by extremists of the Third Estate was established. The king became effectively a powerless pawn. A terrifying mob emerged, manipulated at will by the intellectuals of the new system.

Many people in England welcomed these developments; Burke did not. His *Reflections on the Revolution in France*, though published as early as 1790, predicted that the outcomes would be bloody, predicted the murder of the Royal Family, predicted the militarism and ideological instability of the regime and the way it would devour its own children and even its replacement in due course by the dictatorship of a military adventurer. History was soon to furnish Burke's predictive account with an uncanny factual endorsement. There were the terrible revolutionary wars the French imposed on their neighbours, the mass murder of the Royal Family and the nobility, as well as the internecine strife among the revolutionary fanatics themselves, with many of them too going to the guillotine. Finally, in due course came the emergence of Napoleon, who quelled the murderous atmosphere but in turn was to sacrifice millions of innocents in Europe to his ruthless and cynical military and political ambition.

The French Revolution as the 'Crucial Event of Modern History'

Even in its infancy, McCue remarks, Burke had seen in the French upheaval 'the crucial event of modern history' (McCue

1997: 25). Clearly, this was not a happy conclusion. From our later vantage point, while we may see more to the French Enlightenment than just the Revolution, we can also see that the latter was quite clearly the prime product of the new thinking. Given that Burke's faith in God and in divine providence informs all his thoughts and writings, it was inevitable that he would find that new thinking repugnant. We know, moreover, what Burke could not have known. We know he *understated* the ills released. We know that the moral descent in human affairs which the French experience constituted, according to Burke, was not a one-off anomaly. After the nineteenth-century lull, the twentieth century brought to birth vastly worse versions of the horrors which the French Enlightenment and Revolution had loosed on the world. Again, an extended discussion must wait until Chapter 4.

Burke's English Anxieties over French Events

Early on in *Reflections*, Burke makes clear his *English* anxieties as to French woes. The whole French experiment is widely supported in certain *learned* quarters and certain high places in England, says Burke. The people concerned include both men of the cloth and laymen. This information is conveyed to the reader within a very few pages from the beginning.[11] Since the book identified the revolutionary dangers almost from the start, perhaps it deserves – this side of idolatry, of course – the accolades it has received from admirers of its perspicacity. Burke was very alarmed at the weak power in relation to the executive and the armed forces of the reconstituted French Assembly. It seems extraordinary that so many readers in Burke's day missed this crucial consideration. Has any scholar, any writer, ever articulated the essence of the French Revolution and of the totalitarian offspring it was later to spawn, as well as Burke?

(T)he National Assembly find themselves in a state of the greatest humiliation. . . . With a compelled appearance of deliberation, they vote under the dominion of a stern necessity . . . they have their residence in a city whose constitution has emanated neither from the charter of their king, nor from their legislative power. There they are surrounded by an army not raised either by the authority of their crown, or by their command; and which, if they should order to dissolve itself, would instantly dissolve them. . . . There a majority, sometimes real, sometimes pretended, captive itself, compels a captive king to issue as royal edicts, at third hand, the polluted nonsense of their most licentious and giddy coffee-houses. It is notorious, that all their measures are decided before they are debated. (Burke 1790: 41–2)

The Drive to Evil is Dominated by a Section of the Educated Classes

Burke seems particularly perspicacious in his understanding of the way the different strata of society interact when there is severe or radical disruption of the social and political order. It would seem a commonplace that in any society the social whole is at times menaced by the independently coarse and brutal behaviour of some of the lowest members of society. More important is that Burke also understands that the drive to political error, which may also be realized in *actual* evil, often comes from much nearer the top of society, often from ostensibly well-educated individuals and groups, whose speculative abstractions often burden and harass us, sometimes deliberately and sometimes by mistake. These top people often include, of course, ruffians risen from below, as was the case with Hitler and Stalin.

Burke understands such political sociology well, as does the French political theorist, Benjamin Constant, a few decades younger than Burke, who was described in Chapter 1 as a kind of French equivalent of Burke. The stuff of political nightmare is given when fatal ideology is bonded to mob ignorance. Burke conveys all the atmosphere of the grisly dialectic between the two:

> Amidst assassination, massacre, and confiscation, perpetrated or meditated, they are forming plans for the good order of future society. Embracing in their arms the carcases of base criminals, and promoting their relations on the title of their offences, they drive hundreds of virtuous persons to the same end, by forcing them to subsist by beggary or by crime.
>
> The Assembly, their organ, acts before them the farce of deliberation. . . . They act like the comedians of a fair before a riotous audience; they act amidst the tumultuous cries of a mixed mob of ferocious men, and of women lost to shame. (Ibid: 42)

Moreover, to repeat a crucial point, the evil of elites is always conjoined with that of the worst elements of the lower classes. The interactions in times of upheaval between fanatics high in the structures of power and often themselves of bourgeois or even aristocratic background, and their henchmen, the most brutal villains of the lowest stratum, was a notable feature of the French Revolution. The same phenomenon, but more generalized, was also apparent in the frequent political use by the leadership of a frenzied mob, described above with astonishingly evocative terror and horror by Burke, though he had not actually witnessed it. And the ideological cement, as we might call it, is the theorizing and moralizing engaged in by the philosophers of whatever at a given moment constitutes the New Order.

The notion of the given moment of a New Order is entirely apposite. The Revolution, as it unfolds and is further exposed to our gaze by Burke's startling account, is not so much a single and unchanging entity as a series of entities, the latest mutating as soon as it has taken shape into yet another manifestation. Burke's sense of the potential menace in France arises from his having spotted what O'Brien calls the 'ferocious dynamic' of the Revolution. Burke is therefore not taken in by the peaceful lull of 1790, which misled so many people as to the drift of events in France.

Burke's Religious Anxiety at the Turn of Events

Burke was opposed to the abstract, rationalistic, a-historical thinking of the Enlightenment. The vital task is to give a just account of what Burke saw as the terrible constitutional and moral dangers brought upon humanity's head by the one-dimensional, yet inflated and pretentious political philosophy propagated, for domestic use and for export alike, not only but especially by many of the intellectuals of eighteenth-century France. The secular program was infused with anti-Christian sentiment, in the French case by definition a hostility to the Catholic Church.

Burke was offended by what he saw as this French impiety. He claimed of the English that 'the majority of the people of England, far from thinking a religious national establishment unlawful, hardly think it lawful to be without one' (ibid.: 61). In England, such attitudes could also hide behind a conventional anti-Catholicism. Within a very few pages of its opening Burke's *Reflections* advances a striking and unambiguously religious metaphor to express his alarm at the current proceedings in France and the activities of certain English thinkers, including Churchmen, who welcomed and sought to imitate such goings-on:

> The beginnings of confusion with us in England are at present feeble enough; but with you, we have seen an infancy still more feeble, growing by moments into a strength to heap mountains upon mountains, and to wage war with Heaven itself. (Burke 1993: 9)

Such troublemakers were, by definition, a missionary force, not confined to their native land, and Burke therefore much condemned their English sympathizers and acolytes. For example, in England, there was 'The Revolution Society' which existed officially to celebrate the Great Settlement. In Burke's day it had been led to pursue anti-popery and an admiration for the Revolution in France, by the likes of the Reverent Dr Richard Price, a dissenting clergyman. In November 1789, the Society published a pamphlet welcoming the French upheaval, in terms of anti-Catholicism. A vote of congratulations was also addressed to the National Assembly in Paris which warmly welcomed it. Burke was appraised of all this the following January and by the following November had published his *Reflections*.

The Political and Moral Arguments of *Reflections*

Reflections appeals to justice, pity and piety as well as to probity, both religious and secular.[12] Burke speaks of the French National Assembly's 'contempt of moral' and 'defiance of economical principles' (Burke 1790: 141). He deplores the Assembly's decision to put 'church booty . . . at the disposal of the nation' (Ibid). He further deplores the huge sums of paper money issued against the security of this plundered property (Ibid). And he deprecates the callous irresponsibility of all this destruction:

> Who but the most desperate adventurers in philosophy and finance could at all have thought of destroying the settled revenue of the state, the sole security for the public credit, in the hope of rebuilding it with the materials of confiscated property? (Ibid)

The spite and malice of the Revolution and its friends is worse still. Dr Price, he of the 'Revolution Society', is mentioned repeatedly in *Reflections*. It is his cruel exultation at the fall of King Louis, a cruelty akin to that of the Paris rabble, which seems most to have angered Burke. Of Louis' fate, Burke says: 'I shall be led with great difficulty to think he deserves the cruel and insulting triumph of Paris, and of Dr. Price' (ibid.: 51) and again: 'If it could have been made clear to me, that the king and queen of France . . . were inexorable and cruel tyrants . . . I should think their captivity just' (Ibid).

The central political message of *Reflections* is that political change for the sake of change is a dangerous folly. Necessary change has two functions, which are interrelated. First, it aims to remove significant blemishes and flaws in political arrangements. Second, it aims to preserve the integrity of the system as a whole. Burke believed, with certain reservations, that France had possessed a relatively decent society, which mainly through the vanity of her philosophers, was carelessly undone. When a society has a decent *constitution*, by which word Burke means, not a single document specifying the political principles regulating the society as a whole, but a set of overall political arrangements which the test of time has shown to be effective, the first priority of politics should be to maintain their integrity. Near the end of *Reflections*, Burke spells out his view in the simplest clarity. 'I would not exclude alteration . . . but even when I changed, it should be to preserve' (ibid.: 148). This stipulation alone makes it clear that Burke must inevitably denounce the events in France.

Reflections appeals to the realities of history and tradition and the demands that particular histories make on particular peoples. Worshippers of reason detached from the realities of history, regarding themselves as possessed of Olympian insight, France's self-appointed saviours of humanity were for Burke a deadly threat to European civilization. Bredvold and Ross, however, insist that Burke does not mount a defence of history against reason. On the contrary, they say, he was perhaps above all a *defender* of reason. What he hated was *over-reliance* on reason, the construction of a whole system of ideas from first principles in disregard of historical and present realities (Bredvold and Ross: 5).

Burke called such over-reliance 'rationalism', though in our day the word tends to mean no more than a sensible reliance on clear thought and sound evidence along with reasonable assumptions and inferences. How far short of Burke's prescriptions the French ideologues have fallen is a theme never far from his mind. The reader senses his pity and outrage at the ill-treatment of the king, 'a mild and lawful monarch' (Burke 1790: 25). He found such behaviour and the restless and rootless politics inspiring it 'unnatural'. For his rhetoric's sake Burke called the perpetrators 'the French' though he knew most French people, rich and poor alike, were innocent and paid the price, and a heavy one:

> Laws overturned; tribunals subverted; industry without vigour; commerce expiring; the revenue unpaid, yet the people impoverished; a church pillaged, and a state not relieved; civil and military anarchy made the constitution of the kingdom; every thing human and divine sacrificed to the idol of public credit, and national bankruptcy the consequence. (Ibid)

Burke's Extraordinary Perspicacity

O'Brien speaks of Burke's powers of political dissection as demonstrated in Reflections in the most glowing terms conceivable:

> The grand distinguishing feature of the *Reflections* is the power of Burke's insight into the character of the French Revolution, then at an early stage. (Burke in O'Brien 1997: 215)

Readers will perhaps remember that O'Brien offers Burke substantially the same praise for his very first book, *A Vindication of Natural Society*, in which instance the young Burke's perspicacity had been such as to discern the adverse aspects of the Enlightenment at an early point of its development. None of this, neither his early nor his late perceptiveness, is to say that Burke rejected *all* revolutions. And as we saw in the first chapter and will see in the next, many authorities are far from seeing him as the genius O'Brien identifies. Nor do Burke's views in *Reflections* or anywhere else signal hostility to enlightened thinking and behaviour, in the old-fashioned sense of 'enlightened'.

The Characteristic Facts of A Priori Thinking

Burke also insistently draws our attention to inexorable facts, both of the world we live in and of the life of the mind. Purely a priori reflection, however elevated the intentions which employ it, almost always entails sentimental abstractions lacking any safe anchorage in experience. Burke is hostile to 'any abstract plan of government or of freedom' (Burke 1790: 24). Mitchell says Burke was able to predict the Terror of 1792–4 because the governing and a priori assumptions of the revolutionaries were always flawed and unviable (Mitchell 1993: xv). It follows directly that the proper business of politics is neglected.

Reflections points to the consequences of these unattached abstractions in the form of faction-manipulated brutality, mob-rule and ruthless political dictatorship. Burke takes fundamental moral issue with:

all those, who, attending only to the shell and husk of history, think they are waging war with intolerance, pride, and cruelty, whilst, under color of abhorring the ill principles of antiquated parties, they are authorizing and feeding the same odious vices in different factions, and perhaps in worse. (Burke 1790: 85)

The most obvious examples surround and suffuse those watchwords of the French Revolution, *Liberty*, *Equality* and *Fraternity*.

Burke had long before the French tumult argued, for example, that liberty, as a mere concept taken without qualification, is practically meaningless. It has to be linked to concrete realities, in the British and American case, for example, to safeguards such as ultimate electoral control of taxation (Burke 1775 in Canavan 1960: 7–8).

What is true of liberty is also true of other political goods. Burke believes, for example, in monarchy, and holds that monarchy is perfectly compatible with liberty. Monarchy too, however, must be limited. Burke thus declares for 'freedom under a *qualified* monarchy' (McCue 1997: 28).

Neither is Burke impressed with 'equality'. He speaks disparagingly of 'a pretended natural equality in man' (ibid.: 114). Burke urges on humankind:

> the happiness that is to be found by virtue in all conditions; in which consists the true moral equality of mankind, and not in that monstrous fiction, which, by inspiring false ideas and vain expectations into men destined to travel in the obscure walk of laborious life, serves only to aggravate and imbitter that real inequality, which it never can remove; and which the order of civil life establishes as much for the benefit of those whom it must leave in an humble state, as those whom it is able to exalt to a condition more splendid. (Burke 1790: 23)

Burke repudiated the casting aside of long-established behaviour, relationships and institutions as if they were worn out and dispensable therefore at will. Addressing the young Parisian admirer whose letters to Burke sparked off the *Reflections*, Burke said of the folly of the French as he saw it:

> You had all these advantages in your ancient states; but you chose to act as if you had never been moulded into civil society and had everything to begin anew. You began ill, because you began by despising everything that belonged to you. (Ibid: 22)

Burke was an intransigent opponent of deliberate comprehensive change, whether this was political, social, moral or religious in form. He favoured, that is to say, what in the twentieth
century Karl Popper called 'piece-meal' reform (Popper 1960).
We repeat that his most crucial opposition was to large-scale
theoretical schemes, often at base sentimental abstractions,
lacking any historically or practically rooted conviction. Though
he was a scourge of immoral or inhumane practices, he always
favoured the repair of inadequate arrangements or even of
iniquitous ones, to root and branch upheaval. In modern
language we could say he admired and banked on reformation
and adaptation when present arrangements were demonstrably
inadequate or immoral. Thus Burke was never a rigid theorist or
practitioner of politics.

Politics and Divine Providence

The political question for Burke, as this book has constantly
argued, was not simply the nature of politics as a purely human
phenomenon. Unlike the revolutionaries and the philosophers
of the French Enlightenment, Burke did not see politics as
a product of the human genius in an *autonomous* sense. We are,
so to speak, under instruction. As we saw earlier in this chapter,
Burke took even the humblest prudential rules of politics as
falling under God's guidance (Burke 1796 in Canavan 1960: 14).
He believed that proper politics was the obedient enactment,
at the feeble human level, of the divinely given order of the
universe. Burke also disagreed with the French Enlightenment's
politics, *procedurally*. For Burke, governance secured by religious faith does not operate politically like the large, inflated
dogmas of the Enlightenment. That is to say that it does not
all the time, or even usually, summon up a grand morality of
political practice.

On the contrary, for Burke, politics, for all its manifest complexity, is often the pursuit of the ordinary and un-dramatic.

That is to say that the very portentousness of the French philosopher-politicians was an element in their undoing. We have
seen that he hated what he called 'metaphysical' thinking.[13]
All Burke's life he had maintained the view that fundamental
questions of social and political theory should *not* be raised if
they can possibly be avoided (Canavan 1960: 68). Indeed, it was
the *soi-disant* sceptics of the Enlightenment, especially in France,
who thought of politics generally in terms of lofty moral sentiments and universally binding imperatives, which have to be
brought to bear comprehensively on political life.

Burke regarded these philosopher-politicians with contempt.
Above all he excoriated their vanity, a point made clear in the
searing scorn of some of his remarks about Voltaire (Burke 1790:
128) and even more in those about Rousseau, a man Burke saw
as entirely consumed with vanity and grating self-importance.
Burke's *A Letter to a Member of the National Assembly* contains a
very spirited analysis of the nature of vanity in general and of
Rousseau's dedicated version in particular. It also contains, as
O'Brien points out, a prediction that the French monarch would
be murdered, two years before that heinous crime took place.
Burke also predicts in this magisterial essay, the murder of
Marie-Antoinette, his only error being that she would be slain
first (Burke in O'Brien 1997: 242–4).

Enlightenment Notions of the Natural and the Unnatural

As Francis Canavan says, the French revolutionaries of the 1790s
believed in a natural order, which had been obscured by the
unnatural influence of religion and allied habits of deference
(Canavan 1960: 16). By deliberated planning, enlightened men
could construct a natural order and immutable, universal premises deriving from it. This, however, required a radical break
with the past. One exhortation commending this viewpoint, an
example cited by Burke, was the terrifying speech made by

Rabaud de St Etienne: 'il faut . . . tout détruire; oui tout détruire; puisque tout est à recreer'. [We have to destroy everything, yes destroy everything, since everything has to be made anew].[14] The speaker, as L.G. Mitchell points out, was a Protestant Pastor (Mitchell 1993: xi). The words, however, are surely remote from devout Protestantism of any shade.

One might suggest that such large and cosmic propositions are menacing to Christian souls such as Burke's, since they are uncomfortably close to nihilism, or even worse, to a blasphemous mimicry of the Deity. The notion that the real human being is distorted, warped, hidden by the unnatural influence of an artificial society, and above all by the ministrations of a false and artificial religion, is a central one to the French Enlightenment, made famous by Rousseau's words about our being born free but being everywhere in chains. The contention, if we think about it coolly, suggests that raw nature is preferable to the 'artificial' imperatives and controls of organized society.

At the level of common sense, it hardly seems convincing to link a pre-political nature as the French Enlightenment did, with a vastly ambitious transforming politics. Admittedly, the reader's attention should be drawn to the instability of notions such as 'nature'. Hobbes and Rousseau differ diametrically about the delights of nature. The former has pre-political existence as nasty, brutish and short; the latter has it as an idyllic state, subsequently confiscated from humanity by an artificial order. Few human concepts are as flexible and shifting in meaning as 'nature'. Shakespeare has the most pitiless of all his men of ill-will, Edmund in *King Lear*, pronounce 'Nature' his 'Goddess'.[15] Edmund's unfathomable cynicism and ruthlessness make clear to what an unrefined, unimproved human condition he refers.

In fact, the concept of a pre-social man is meaningless, as we learn from thinkers as far apart as Aristotle, who famously identifies man as a social and political animal, and Montesquieu (McCue 1997: 110).[16] Savagery is not pre-social; it is, as Hobbes says, nasty, brutish and short, however, with the needs of human nature neither properly understood nor met. Edmund really extols a kind of primordial rottenness, with all social bonds cast off. Shakespeare would surely have agreed with Burke that human beings need repeated shaping by the habits of civilized order to become themselves part of that order.

For Burke, as for most conservatives, comprehensive abstract theories have nothing beneficial to deliver. Burke's attitude to the past, present and future, and to the human political condition as a natural phenomenon or otherwise, is intelligible only in relation to his Christian faith. Sound politics for Burke is an obedient response to the will of the Almighty.

Post *Reflections* Writing:
Appeal from the New to the Old Whigs (1791)

The Jesuit philosopher Francis Canavan says that Burke's central thought in religion and in politics was that of order. Behind his conception of social order 'lay always the grand idea of the order of the universe' (Canavan 1960: 19). Canavan refers to Sir Ernest Barker's words: 'The idea of the divine concordance of the Universe, which includes the State in its scheme, haunted the mind of Burke' (Barker 1951 in Canavan 1960: 19). Indeed, as Canavan points out, for Burke it is man's proper nature to live, not in animal barbarism, but under the civilizing constraints of a decent society. Canavan regards a passage in *Appeal from the New to the Old Whigs* as best capturing Burke's view:

> The state of civil society . . . is a state of nature; and much more truly so than a savage and incoherent mode of life. For man is by nature reasonable; and he is never perfectly in his natural state, but where he is placed where reason may be best cultivated, and most predominates. Art is man's nature. We are as much at least in a state of nature in formed manhood, as in immature and helpless infancy. (Burke 1791: 205)

Burke's Christian Politics Re-emphasized

Burke had all his life to dissemble somewhat in matters of religion. His mind was for all that fundamentally a Christian one. Canavan maintains that, according to Christian orthodoxy, the doctrine of the Creation entails that the created universe, in every detail of its course and evolution, depends on the Creator. It follows that the actions of all creatures, even the free actions of men, are fully subject to God's dominion and direction (Canavan 1960: 178). Canavan freely admits that the reconciliation of human freedom and Divine omnipotence is a profound problem in metaphysics and theology. It is not, he says, however, one which engaged the mind of Edmund Burke. Nor need it detain the scholarly pursuit of Burke's politics (Ibid).

Burke frequently refers to divine providence; indeed Canavan believes there was no Christian doctrine he believed in more profoundly. He assumes, rather than seeks to explain the doctrine (ibid.: 178–9). While Burke's views on everyday politics are grittily pragmatic, however, and while he maintained a deep suspicion of over-intellectualized schemes of human advancement, he also believed in more urgent, incomparably more complex and higher authorities than those appealed to by the sceptics, French or English. He believed in a divine order beyond this world which nevertheless laid down imperatives for the political management of this one. Burke mostly spoke of the politics of this world; this does not mean he was not profoundly aware of the imperatives of another. Professor Grant has interpreted him, perhaps rightly, as not very religious in observance (Grant 1986). Even so, in the next chapter, we will disagree with Grant on the matter of Burke's faith and his understanding of providence.

Providence, for unbelievers a chimera, and even for reverent doubters, those pilgrims of modernity, hovering at the edge of faith, at best a mostly invisible text, of which a glimpse may be caught in rare moments of grace, is to the cradle Christian like Burke as obvious as night and day. If we may change the comparison, the truths of Christianity, to people of Burke's disposition, are as clear as what the ancients called 'the music of the spheres', the ultimate coherence and order in the universe, was to its initiates. Burke would thus agree with Hamlet that: 'There is a Divinity that shapes our ways, roughhew them how we will'.[17]

Burke shows that portentous abstractions, while they are for the most part very lacking in useful virtuous content, are vibrant with positive menace. Indeed, 'nature' is one such insidious notion. Burke notes very particularly that various catchwords on the one hand, and unnecessary and pseudo-scientific plans on the other, are based on the articulations of celebrated scholars, at the time of his writing, mostly French ones: Voltaire, Rousseau, Condorcet, in particular (M[c]Cue 1997: 109).[18]

Burke, Respect for Our Ancestors and the Need for Hierarchy

Applauding a reverent care for the past, for tried, tested political institutions and practices, Burke says that neglect of the national past is extremely dangerous, both to the present generation and to its progeny. Burke warns specifically that: 'People will not look forward to posterity who never look backward to their ancestors' (Burke 1993: 33). Respect for the past is part of the hierarchy of order and respect in society.

The author's account of the Revolution in France combines a disgust for the ill-treatment even of the meanest or lowliest of human beings, with an insistence on the need for hierarchy in human society and for a necessary concentration of authority lodged with the upper classes, especially the aristocracy. The most crucial thing about the book, as we shall see, is the way it epitomizes Burke's opinions across the whole corpus of his writings, though he says many important things elsewhere which he does not treat in *Reflections*.

Burkean Polemic and Rhetoric and the Enlightenment

Reflections is famous for its polemical character. Burke was nothing if not a polemicist, though he was vastly more than just a polemicist. The work is also often thought of in terms of high blown rhetoric. Though there are passages of grandiose rhetoric, these do not predominate, says O'Brien (O'Brien 1997: 218). The book is a work of political scholarship, one might even say a principled analysis of political cause and effect, on realist, even Machiavellian lines, though Machiavelli is an entirely secular figure according to standard accounts. Burke had clearly discerned the central fact, the driving and insatiable ideology, what O'Brien calls 'the ferocious dynamic', of the revolution in France. If we do X a broadly determinable Y will follow.

Burke's greatest book, at least as it is usually regarded, opens with a Christian infused account of the Revolution in France, an afflatus in a real sense defined for him by its impiety. This does not mean that Burke was against the Enlightenment[19] in the sense that he opposed policies of reform. His frequent support, even ardent support, for reform, in turn does not mean that politics should be conducted via the pulpit. On the contrary, in its warnings about the French spectre now stalking the English political landscape, *Reflections* specifically insists that it should not. 'No sound ought to be heard in the church but the healing voice of Christian charity' (Burke 1790: 11–12). We saw earlier that Burke's whole political career was aimed at combining the reproduction of the best aspects of our traditional way of life with improvements to that way of life brought about by reforms.

For Burke, Mercy and Justice Are Inseparable

McCue notes that Burke saw mercy and justice as inseparable. Without mercy justice is impossible (McCue 1997: 62). This is recognized, of course, both in our Common Law and in the

European derivatives of Roman law. It is significant that Albert Camus, who perhaps never read Burke, but was very much a soul-mate in his espousal of a politics of limits, called Karl Marx 'the prophet of justice without mercy'. Such are the interesting links in intellectual history, when a twentieth-century French atheist, through his espousal of decency, echoes, however inadvertently, a passionate eighteenth-century Irish Christian in his defence of charity. For Burke, as Francis Canavan puts it, 'The moral law finds its archetype in God, for it is derived from "that eternal, immutable law in which reason and will are the same"' (Burke 1790 in Canavan 1960: 21).

Burke's Preference for Landed Wealth

We noted in the first chapter and have reaffirmed in this that Burke believes in a fundamentally aristocratic political dispensation, an order of landed property such as had predominated for centuries and been reaffirmed by the Great Settlement of the 1690s. Burke thinks that there is something ennobling and enduring about the land itself. It will probably not have escaped the attention of readers that this prejudice is still alive and well. We will give it some attention in Chapter 3. The nearest French equivalent to Burke in this regard was Benjamin Constant. Some thirty years younger than Burke, Constant persistently praises agrarian-based wealth as superior to commercial or manufacturing-based wealth. The bias of both men was being upstaged, certainly in the British context, since aristocratic and bourgeois wealth were in fact merging, beginning their long and still-fertile contribution to human welfare, as mediated by successful market economies. On those developments Burke could not have known about, his voice must necessarily be silent.

The Intellectual Force of Burke's Political Views

This is a huge question over which scholars have disagreed profoundly in the past and over which they remain very much divided. We saw in Chapter 1, the huge divisions in the appraisals different writers have made of the man, ranging from admiration to sneering contempt. This is not surprising. Burke is a writer of great power and intellect but his audience is first and foremost a political rather than an academic one. He is writing more about political problems than about political explanation. The two are intertwined, of course, but it is beyond doubt that the works are mostly policy-oriented. Those who oppose Burke's theorizing are likely to oppose it all the more because it is a politically engaged theorizing. To this difficulty arising from a kind of ambivalence as to what the subject matter is addressing, we must add the further difficulty caused by the richness and complexity of the prose and its conceptual content.

The complexity is not surprising. There is rich variety informing what Burke thinks. He is a Christian, although not noisily so. He is emphatically a conservative and he is also clearly a classical liberal in David Conway's understanding of the term (Conway 2004). It is clear that Burke marks out for himself a position quite distinct in the discussion of nature and of what is natural to man. He does not agree with the Hobbes notion of a 'state of nature of primordial savagery such that man's life is 'nasty, brutish and short'. Nor, on the other hand, does he see human potential as blocked by an oppressive and transcendable order, as Marx and his many predecessors and successors do. Nor does he see civilization attained, as did Hayek, by a fundamentally artificial moral learning alien to human nature. His view resembles that of Emile Durkheim, despite the temporal and religious gulf between them. Both men insist that our humankind is socially formed and that the nature of men and women cannot be dreamed of, much less identified, outside real, concrete social practices.

Durhkeim is the secular and Burke the Christian intelligence. Burke believes that our natural passions (i.e. feelings) are implanted in us by the Deity. As Canavan says, and as we have already pointed out, his theory of the basis of morals in the natural affections bears an obvious resemblance to Adam Smith's *Theory of the Moral Sentiments* (Canavan 1960: 56). Burke holds that our instincts are right when they are directed by reason. The relationship between our natural feelings and morals depends on the divine creation of human nature. God is the author of human nature and of its instinctive moral response to basic moral values (Canavan 1960: 55–6).

It might be said that Burke catches both the shortcomings of the human race, to the extent that he is a pessimist, and the glories of human potential, to the extent that, optimistically, he applauds in us the redemptive powers which he takes to be of divine origin. Burke approved of the embrace England had offered or originally enforced on her Celtic neighbours, and though he was very critical of the English Protestant ascendancy in Ireland, he never supported separatist movements in the country of his birth. By definition he could not have found favour with any Irish entanglement with the Revolution in French affairs.

The Enlightenment Is Not Homogenous and Should Not Be Airily Dismissed

It would be absurd and improper, however, to dismiss the whole Enlightenment. We can agree with Burke, as we ponder his analysis in Reflections, that it had a disastrous effect in France. It was the blanket rejection of the human past which was so opposed by Burke. Burke considers history 'a great improver of the understanding from which much political wisdom may be learned' (Burke 1803–27 in Canavan 1960: 12).

We must make distinctions both between places and persons. We should note the differences between the French case on the one hand and the English and Scottish version on the other. We must note too that the French Enlightenment itself contains such models of moral and intellectual clarity and integrity as Jean-Baptiste Say and Benjamin Constant. Slightly later, comes the excellent and morally refined work of the Catholic economist, Frédéric Bastiat.

The English and Scottish Enlightenment, by contrast with the French, is *mostly* benign and often brilliant, featuring the powerful, innovative writings of giants like David Hume and Adam Smith. Smith is widely regarded as the greatest economist of the Scottish Enlightenment, and probably of the movement as a whole. From the writings of Smith and other great economists, humanity has evolved a superior management of economic problems than was available to earlier times. Our brief reflection on Smith makes nonsense of any attempt to represent Burke as a reactionary. The two men were intimate friends. Burke was clearly in no way opposed to new or path-breaking thinking in political economy.

The Enlightenment, Subtraction and Abstraction: Some General Discussion

One thing the Enlightenment in its French version did was to pull down the pillars of the Christian temple. This was its subtraction, what it removed from the European intellectual universe. French Catholicism was dealt a blow from which it has never recovered, from which perhaps it will never recover.

The thought of the French Enlightenment, however, was suspect to Burke not only in its dethronement of Christianity and the Deity; it also relied too much on secular abstraction, on lofty vagaries. The mischievous habit it added to Europe's intellectual life, was a now all too familiar abstract sentimentality. We cannot dismiss these abstractions all simply as talk, however. Their consequences were too vast and painful for that. The talk had a programme, and a vicious one as we now know to our cost.

The Dangers of Mere Words

Burke knew what was wrong with the talk and the programme. For him the new thinking was not sufficiently grounded in practical materialism, in the real and concrete issues of this life. It postured, it spouted, rather than dealt with realities. Burke possessed most unusual powers of language, both in the oratorical and in the literary sense. He knew all too well, however, that words as such are cheap. They may be empty or malignant; they may hide or dissemble. One might therefore say that for Burke, political dispensations are not to be judged only by their words, by how and what they declaim, but even more by how they live, by how their subjects or citizens are treated as a result of their particular arrangements for human governance.[20]

For the Enlightenment in France, certainly for its best-known representatives, the most proper people to teach the world how to live were its most distinguished intelligences. No appeal should be made to any authority other than educated humanity itself. Superstition and personal Gods were declared redundant. Many of the luminaries called themselves 'Deists', signalling a belief in God but not in a *personal* God. In France, in particular, atheism proper also became quite common among the intellectuals. We know that David Hume, himself a sceptic, was quite shocked at the avowed atheism of many French thinkers he met in France (Clayton, Blackburn and Carroll 2006: 115, 212). The Enlightenment, Deist or atheist, was a conscious movement to replace the ideas of Christianity and of divine providence, with a reliance on a secular, purely human intellection.

Burke can be seen, from the beginnings of his published writings to the penning near the end of his life of his most famous work, to have regarded this Enlightenment aspiration as the most dangerous hubris (Burke 1982). His *Reflections* is the most notable work ever written making this question the central focus. It is an impassioned attack both on a philosophical crusade which Burke thought a vast exercise in human pride and on the 'Revolution in France' – as Burke called what is usually referred to as the 'French Revolution' – which was for him that crusade's first poisoned fruit. This two-pronged attack, on Enlightenment and Revolution, was very far from being the sole focus of his writings, but it will appear from our historical vantage point, perhaps even more than it seemed from his, the most important one. The other main focus of his work was his explanation and defence of what we may call the English or British way of politics.

Burke's attack on the worst aspects of Enlightenment thinking should not surprise us. Such an attack is generated from his defence of what he loved and admired. The political life of his adopted land had been tested by the centuries, experienced and felt and approved by those who lived under it as much as by those who presided over it. That a challenge to that life should have dominated Burke's most famous book can scarcely surprise us. After all, we have seen far more of the dire consequences of this intended substitution than Burke did. Chapter 4 will deal with some of these consequences, outcomes even more terrible than those Burke was able to describe or imagine.

The noisiest and most influential voices in France are undoubtedly those of Voltaire and Rousseau, though neither was alive to witness the outcome of the corruption they had introduced. Rousseau, indeed, can make some claim to being the most influential thinker of recent centuries, with a profound influence on totalitarian theories and practice. He is also without doubt the most influential theorist of education of modernity, arguably of all time, the man who invented what conservatives regard as the disastrous philosophy of 'progressive' education. In Chapter 4, our dealing with the relevance of Burke today, will necessarily also involve our grappling with the ghost of the brilliant, but also malignant Swiss egotist.

Burke as a Teacher

We should add that despite his love of flowing and magisterial rhetoric, and his pre-eminence in its use, indeed a command of complex language which would defeat the uneducated, Burke was, and surely at least in some sense deliberately, a marvellous teacher. It is surprising how rarely even the longest of his complex sentences defeat the attentive reader, such was the shining clarity that illumines his words. Like most distinguished writers, however, he favoured simplicity of terms when it came to conclusions and the spelling out of policies. This is a strategy calculated to make the deepest friends of some and the most intransigent enemies of others. Nothing is more offensive to those who would circumscribe human freedoms than the combination of brilliant argument and clear conclusion which defines Burke's writings. In Chapter 3, in our discussion of the reception Burke has met, we will bring out the curtness his opponents resort to. We will also take especial pains to stress how wrongly even many of Burke's favourably inclined readers have taken, not his conclusions, but the basis of his reasoning.

3

Great Acclaim, Some Derision and Much Controversy: How Burke Has Been Received

Introduction

It has fallen to no individual in history to be universally revered. To be remembered at all is to be part of an exceptional group, it being true for better or worse that the humble majority of humankind is mostly extinguished by the passing of time. It is also part of the standard experience of history, however, that even the greatest and most remarkable men and women are sometimes forgotten. Certainly no one ever receives universal acclaim. And in this last respect, Burke is no exception. He has been showered with unstinting praise and, though much less commonly, with strikingly contemptuous obloquy, as we saw in Chapter 1.

The *range* of reaction to Burke continues to be vast, though very much more favourable than hostile. Often it is implicit. Simon Schama we have already cited for his very well received work on the French Revolution in which Burke is treated as an irrelevance (Schama 1991). The historian of ideas, Robert Grant, by contrast, could scarcely be more specific in his praise, saying (that) 'In some ways Burke is the greatest of all political thinkers; incidentally, the only one of first-rate importance, apart from Machiavelli, who was also a working statesman' (Grant 1986).

There is no doubt of Burke's success in terms of readership and sales. It was made clear in Chapters 1 and 2 that many of his writings, across his entire working life, reached a wide and appreciative readership. He was extraordinarily well-known *before* he published *Reflections*, and after a somewhat shaky start into which we will later delve a little, his most famous book made him a world figure in the literature and history of political thinking.

On the sales of *Reflections*, Stanlis presents us with some mostly unadorned figures. The first British edition sold 12,000 copies in the first month. In less than a year there were eleven editions. By 1796 over 30,000 official copies had been sold. At a time when books circulated widely and were often read in public to large groups, this was, says Stanlis, in the only admiring comment he allows himself on the achievement, 'phenomenal' (Stanlis 1991: 39). Today we can surely see Burke's commentary on the French Revolution as numbered amidst the best received books of all time.

In other ways, however, the reception of Burke's analytical output amounts to a notable illustration of the uncertainties in the welcome given to intellectual as to other achievement. For example, though the scholars who have studied him, in his day and since, much more often admire than detest him, we will see in this chapter that it is sometimes far from clear, if we leave aside Burke's manifest intellectual brilliance, *precisely what it is which is being praised.*

Some commentators celebrate both Burke's specific and practically oriented philosophy, *and* his religious persuasion, the latter ultimately inspiring and guiding the former. It may be doubted, however, whether any Burke commentator would deny that the former operates for the most part in terms of a functional autonomy. Most of the time Burke does not need or want to refer to the religious roots of his thinking.

What makes Burke remain controversial, however, is precisely the question of the nature or even the existence of any *ultimate* religious provenance for his views. Even among those who most admire him, there is simply no consensus. The admiration itself is not in doubt. It is the *connections* in Burke's thinking between religion and politics which are problematic.

Burke and Natural Rights

Broadly speaking, Burke is *against* the 'rights' conceived by the Enlightenment and fed directly into political thinking and even into legislation. Such 'rightsology', as it is sometimes sarcastically called today, haunts and muddles us still, as we will see in Chapter 4. Burke is *for* the rights which were embedded in the ancient tradition of Natural Law, rights which derived from a blend of the work of the Greek philosophers and the Hebrew prophets, and were fed by Christianity into politics, mostly by unvoiced but taken for granted *prescription* over the centuries. Burke had an enormous legal and historical erudition. He had an intimate knowledge of Aristotle and Cicero and the early Christian fathers. Indeed his work contains direct and indirect references to Aristotle's *Ethics* and the *Politics* (Stanlis 1991: 9). As to Cicero, Stanlis notes that Burke's writings quote him eleven times and that his speeches often refer to him (ibid.: 10).

When Burke speaks of our natural rights, which he does occasionally, but forcefully, he means God-given rules for the protection of His creation. The a priori rights airily dreamed up and loudly proclaimed by eighteenth-century French philosophers and their imitators, he regards as conceits as dangerous as they are false and superficial. There may, incidentally, be debates as to how *religious* Burke was. Could any man, however, who was not a profound *believer*, write, this side of gross hypocrisy, as follows?

> He who gave our nature to be perfected by our virtue, willed also the necessary means of its perfection. He willed therefore the state; He willed its connexion with the source and original archetype of all perfection. (Burke 1790: 59)

Frank Canavan is very convincing about human rights. He argues that Burke never denied that men have natural rights. But 'natural rights can be conceived of as following upon human nature in whatever state it may exist, and do not necessarily depend upon the hypothesis of a pre-social or pre-political state of nature' (Canavan 1960: 114). In any actual society, rights must be constrained by laws and rules and other contrivances. The right to property is the obvious case (ibid.: 116). In his statement in the *Report on the Lords' Journals* (Burke in 1794 in Todd 1964) Burke says that property is natural but that 'almost everything concerning property is of artificial contrivance' (ibid.). Here he means no more than that property, a right inherent in humanity, needs a conventional structure for its operations. A passage in *Reflections* is very convincing on the way in which our God-given rights are modified by society:

> These metaphysic rights entering into common life, like rays of light which pierce into a dense medium, are, by the laws of nature, refracted from their straight line. Indeed in the gross and complicated mass of human passions and concerns, the primitive rights of men undergo such a variety of refractions and reflections, that it becomes absurd to talk of them as if they continued in the simplicity of their original direction. (Burke 1790: 37)

Canavan insists on the Christian, metaphysical grounds of Burke's thought, but concedes that his dislike of the false metaphysics of the Enlightenment, which he denounces, leads him to understate, or explain insufficiently, the true grounds of his own moral theory and political orientation. Canavan says Burke's 'lack of concern with stating, criticising, and defending the metaphysical presuppositions of his moral and political theory must be regarded as a weakness of his thought' (Canavan 1960: 52–3).

On the other hand he was religious, and Canavan says it is hard to read his private correspondence and then concur with

Lord Acton's judgement that he was 'not even thoroughly sincere in his religious belief' (ibid.: 48). When Burke does speak of 'natural rights' he does indeed mean those which are bestowed on us by God. In his *Tracts on the Popery Laws* (Burke 1761 in Todd 1964) he says that 'a conservation and secure enjoyment of our natural rights is the great and ultimate purpose of civil society' (ibid.: 49).

Burke Is Incontestably Controversial

What has been said so far in this book, adds up to the view that Burke is a deeply controversial figure. This is in no way unusual. Classicists still dispute, not only the respective merits of Plato and Aristotle, but also the precise meanings which each intended. Shakespeare, more acclaimed than any other writer, has his detractors, including Tolstoy and Shaw. Even Christ, whom many writers, Burke among them, have seen as the Divine Word made incarnate, and whom many non-Christians have much admired, has had very many critics. Hostility to Christianity – anxiety over which is central to *Reflections on the Revolution in France* (Burke 1790: 31) – continues to flourish, despite the achievements of the Christian civilization which Burke so strongly defended. This last point – the Western achievement – needs some modest enlargement. It has filled libraries already of course. In Burke's view – visible across his entire output – English/British history exemplified this achievement.

The West and Its Individualism

It is widely recognized today that the uniqueness of the West reflects the Christian emphasis on the individual soul. This doctrine generated the idea of *individualism*, an essential element in the superiority of Western cultural, political and economic arrangements. Without this distinct individualism, the Renaissance, the Enlightenment itself – which in its better dimensions at least is admirable and immensely fecund – and the vast changes in the betterment of human welfare wrought in time by the British Industrial Revolution and its emulators, would all have been impossible. This all constitutes a causal sequence admitted even by sceptics like Kenneth Minogue. Indeed, Professor Minogue's argument is very emphatic (Minogue 2003). Yet across the centuries, the hostility to the Christian message persists.

The French Enlightenment, for example, essentially though not universally, was deeply anti-Christian. So were its subsequent, fantastical offspring. Communism, for example, was obsessively anti-Christian in inspiration and very often in practice, until a mix of ideological apathy and governmental arthritis set in, and the persecution abated with it. It still lives on, this religious intolerance, in the hybrid Communist/Market society of China. The shorter-lived Nazi version of totalitarianism, it is true, directed its neurotic hatreds against European Jewry in the main and the first instance, but Nazi ideology was also virulently anti-Christian. Indeed, Paul Johnson regards the Nazis as even more anti-Christian than the Communists (Johnson 1982: 482–94). It seems hard to doubt that the destruction of Christianity was on the Nazi agenda as well as integral to the Marxist prospectus.

Burke's Predictive Acumen as to the Horrors to Come

Burke could have known nothing directly about Communism and Nazism, of course, but, as a defender of Christian civilization, he was well aware of, and disposed to warn the world about, the huge moral dangers unleashed by the French *philosophes* and their abstract conceits, particularly their disdain for Christianity. These dangers are made quite apparent in *Reflections*. Moreover, as Professor Grant points out, Burke's forebodings achieve an even more terrifying intensity in his last work, what Grant calls his 'awesome' *Letters on a Regicide Peace* (1796*a*). In Grant's words the text constitutes an

> apocalyptic, nightmare vision of lawless, relentless power, a horrible inversion of the hitherto 'natural' order in civilized states. Here coercion dispenses with allegiance, as do requisition and extortion with exchange. (Grant 1986: 6)

Burke's own characterization of the new French government is to the point. He stresses the deliberateness and intolerance of it all. Burke's use of the word 'design' is manifestly well chosen and deliberate: 'The design is wicked, immoral, impious, oppressive' (Burke 1796*a*: 16). From the same page Grant picks out a masterly characterization by Burke, *avant la lettre*, of the very essence of the aspirations we have come to know as totalitarian.

> The will, the wish, the want, the liberty, the toil, the blood of individuals, is as nothing . . . The State is all-in-all. (Ibid.)

In the 1790s, then, in his last great book and his last set of essays, in what is surely one of the most remarkable intellectual feats in history, Burke, with incomparable acuity, had detected in the rise of French antinomianism, the embryo of far worse horrors to come.

The Foresight of Heine

The remark of the German poet/philosopher Heine in 1842, that the future smelt of Russian leather and many whippings and that his generation's grandchildren had better be born with very thick skins on their backs (Heine 1842), put some more flesh on the nightmarish bones, but by his time the antinomian outpourings had enjoyed forty years more of development,[1] and accordingly supplied Heine with more detail with which to speculate. Heine certainly catches the likelihood of Russia's being involved and a sense of the cruelty in store. It is Burke, though, who seems from our vantage point the truly inspired prophet of the woes which the prideful sins of eighteenth-century France had laid up for the world.

Nor would the retribution for these sins be confined to their Gallic birthplace. Indeed, very many countries were to suffer much worse from them than did France. Burke's anxiety, of course, is that his beloved England might be similarly infected. We can also read in Burke's explorations of late eighteenth-century French politics, given that the poor and the humble did not play a part except in mob agitation, the clear message that it is the glittering elites of position and talent who most need watching.

There are in all societies potentially fatal currents of hatred and revenge and murder swirling around the body politic. They must not be given vent. Nor must they be adopted by clever and influential people. If such people do adopt them, they may subvert their own society first, and may well turn next to those of their neighbours. Burke knew it and said it and it all came true. Nor has the world yet pulled itself clear of the chaos released by the careless intellection, the promiscuous ideology, which Burke so detested. To take the most obvious example: consider the dire consequences of the veneration given Marx's shade and other malicious ghosts. Their having been given so exalted a reception, in so many places in the twentieth century, has spelt the ruin of whole societies, and even in free societies, of many universities.

In this chapter, we must explore more fully the variations in the reception Burke received. We will in some degree be continuing the discussion of our two earlier chapters, that is to say enlarging both on Burke's intellectual output and the public reaction it evoked, since we will be talking of his intellectual *standing* both in his time and subsequently.

The Two Goals of This Chapter

In view of these complex considerations, I have set myself two main, interwoven tasks in this chapter. The first is to try to make further sense of Burke's fundamental understanding of the human place in the scheme of things, including the scheme of things both religious and political, by way of a discussion of the *reception* of his work by his own and subsequent generations. I want to see if we can pin down Burke's fundamental sense of the human and political condition.

The conclusion I have reached and will later try to show more fully, is that whatever the weight of the charges against him of Utilitarianism,[2] it remains true that Burke's politics derives from, and runs parallel to, his religious convictions. It is also true that in some ways Burke leaves the connections between the two problematic. Let us for the moment take the standard view that he was a very convinced Christian. Robert Grant dissents from this claim, in a very perspicacious as well as elegant essay. Burke he says, was notoriously tolerant in religious matters, and even favourably inclined to Hinduism (Grant 1986). These considerations do not seem to imply any lack of religious conviction to me. For the Utilitarians, of course – and Grant is not one – religious affiliation is mostly a polite and politic convention for the maintenance of social order.

Complex Relations and Non-Relations between Religion and Politics

The point, though, is that there are today, as there were in the past, readers and critics favourably disposed to Burke's religion *and* his politics, others favouring neither and yet others favouring one and not the other. We are confronted, then, with a deep ongoing rift in the assessment of the man, in other words with an eminent example of a commonplace thing. Human life is forever characterized by interpersonal ambiguity and contradiction.

It should be reiterated, in particular for those just getting acquainted with this controversial and colourful character that Burke's readers do *not* have to share his Christian views to find his arguments persuasive, just as it is also the case that some Christian believers will not like Burke's secular politics. It is quite clear, indeed, that many present-day Catholic and Protestant *clergy* in the United States and Great Britain and elsewhere will not like Burke's political ideas, or, indeed, his religious views either. His conservatism in both regards will offend them.

It is in any case very important to understand that the Christian provenance of Burke's conservative political beliefs is *not* definitive in explaining those beliefs, which can be held by people whose religion is very different from Burke's, by others who have no religious beliefs at all, or beliefs whose specific religious components remain elusive.

A Magisterial Case in Point: Gibbon on Burke

We may take as a particularly telling example of these last statements the attitude of David Gibbon, one of Burke's most eminent contemporaries, author of the famous *Decline and Fall of the Roman Empire*, a man in religion a sceptic, and now universally regarded as a great historian, indeed, among the most eminent of all time. He much admired *Reflections*, saying of it, with arresting urbanity:

> Burke's book is an admirable protection against the French disease. I admire his eloquence; I approve his politics; I adore his chivalry; and I can almost forgive his reverence for church establishments. (Prior 1854 in Stanlis 1991: 40)

Gibbon's sentiments make it clear that religious scepticism was not confined to France in those years. In fact, however, there is an ongoing continuity here. An ironic, disbelieving attitude to Christianity is still common among the English and increasingly common in America too, though American Christianity remains more robust than is the British case. Among English speakers, however, disbelief is not usually accompanied by an outright hatred of religion of the kind common in eighteenth-century France. This hostility was maintained in the twentieth century by many French writers, of whom Jean-Paul Sartre is the best known. Militant atheism is still exceptional in the case of British or American thinkers, with a few exceptions, such as Oxford's Richard Dawkins, or the scholarly journalist, Christopher Hitchens, who lives in America, though he is British. Gibbon's relaxed scepticism remains the standard for British and American academics who are non-believers.

The Chronology and Character of the Reception Given to Burke

The *second* task of this chapter is to present a broad picture, less of what Burke said, than of the way the world has received his contributions. What Burke said and how he was received, are by definition inextricably related. It is a question of which to emphasize. Necessarily, we have made some of the reception clear already. We have noted how Gibbon warmed to him in the eighteenth century and how Robert Grant has praised him in our day. Obviously, I want to tell the reader more about what Burke said. I also want to show, however, the pattern of praise and disapproval he has received in general terms *as a writer*, that is to say what impression Burke's various works have made for good and ill on their audience.

Inevitably, because *Reflections* has always since its publication been predominant in the discussion of his work, we must devote considerable discussion to the way in which this book has been received, in order to fortify and elaborate what has already been said. This is the book which most captures Burke's reputation, because it is the one which has been most attentively received, though as Grant points out, it cannot stand in for other works

by Burke (Grant 1986: 1). There is much he says in other works
which he does not say in *Reflections*. One of Burke's most outstanding qualities is the fertility of his imagination, which
enabled him to deploy his great learning so effectively across
so many subjects. The writings are vast but various. They do
not come together in an intellectual system. As Grant says, it
is the methods Burke uses, in which he tries to embrace as
many facets of each problem as possible, which constitute his
system (ibid.).

In this chapter, we can advisedly abandon the chronological
structure we imposed on his work in the first two chapters, as we
assessed Burke's ongoing intellectual development. The chronological slant of the present chapter will instead be imposed on
his ongoing *reception* by his own and successive generations. All
this will involve a further account of what he was thought to have
said by various authorities and what your present author thinks
he *actually* said. It may properly be claimed of Burke that he
sometimes needs defending from his friends as much as from
his enemies. Many of those who insist – wrongly – that he is
fundamentally a Utilitarian are also deeply admiring of his
contribution to political knowledge.

Burke: A Reputation Impossible to Ignore?

One thing that neither his contemporaries nor most of those
who followed could do, whether or not they favoured him, was
to ignore Burke, though this is precisely the charge brought
against Simon Schama by Jim McCue (McCue 1997: 11).[3] For
such an eminent scholar as Schama, in his treatment of the
Revolution in eighteenth-century France, one of the crucial
upheavals of modernity, to sideline its most eminent critic, seems
truly weird, and implicitly scornful. Scorn can take explicit
as well as implicit forms, of course. The man whom Macaulay
called the greatest Englishman since Milton, a verdict later
endorsed by John Morley (Morley 2003: 14), Karl Marx was to

dismiss derisively in *Das Kapital* as a bourgeois mouthpiece. Marx was a radical opponent of Burke's thought. In *Das Kapital*, he wrote:

> The sycophant – who in the pay of the English oligarchy played the romantic *laudator temporis acti* [this term from the Roman poet Horace means 'the praiser of the good old days'] against the French Revolution just as, in the pay of the North American colonies at the beginning of the American troubles, he had played the liberal against the English oligarchy – was an out-and-out vulgar bourgeois. (Marx 1976: 925–6).

We will later argue that this latter charge is preposterous, though it was echoed by A.J. P. Taylor, who called Burke 'a Whig hack' which really comes to much the same thing (Taylor 1976: 18). Taylor may well have been repeating it from Marx. Taylor was fond of parading his socialist credentials even at a time – that is to say from the 1960s onwards – when socialism's monstrously erroneous character was becoming more and more obvious. We noted in Chapter 1 the abuse of Burke by these two gentlemen. Taylor can quit our stage now, but we will return to the malicious spirit of Marx both later in this chapter and again in Chapter 4. Let us now consider what Burke's reputation rests on, or perhaps more properly, what it *ought* to rest on.

Burke and the Basis of Reputation

The true basis of intellectual reputation, favourable or adverse, lies in a thinker's demonstrated serious reading, writing and discussion and in how his audience construes these. Burke made prodigious efforts in all three. Inevitably his work has inspired a vast commentary by some very distinguished scholars, often in extensive individual writings. Popular reputation, however, of the kind often absorbed by those who have not read a given writer in much depth, or sometimes even at all, tends to be transmitted by epigrammatic (short, concise) reckonings, or vivid summaries, on the part of notable writers or other persons of high standing, mostly of course those who *have* also evaluated at length the writings in question. Indeed the epigrams and summary viewpoints are often extracted from extensive texts.

Such brevity has its drawbacks, though it does not necessarily lead to false impressions. Before we embark on any detailed textual questions, therefore, for example on the reception accorded to any *particular* writings by Burke, let us look at what epigrammatic remarks and brief commentary have made of Burke's intellectual powers and accomplishments. What did his contemporaries and later commentators on Burke have to say, in terse measure, of his erudition? With what particular intellectual orientation or method did those who admired him connect him? What intellectual deficiencies did his critics find in him? These are questions which can be clarified by summary as well as by elaborate judgement. It is an interesting fact that though he has critics aplenty, they seem to be much outnumbered by his admirers, and this is reflected as much in the overwhelmingly favourable character of these epigrammatic and summary assessments as it is in extended commentary.

Burke: Some Summary Verdicts in Chronological Order

We have already noted the glittering acclaim accorded to Burke by Gibbon. The incontestably brilliant Dr Johnson stood even more in awe of him. 'Burke . . . is such a man, that if . . . you and he stepped aside . . . but for five minutes . . . when you parted, you would say, this is an extraordinary man' (McCue 1997: 16). Charles James Fox paid tribute to Burke's extraordinary intellect, even at a time when they were diverging on the question of the French Revolution (ibid.). In 1794 Coleridge had attacked Burke in a sonnet. In 1797, however, he said in *Biographia Literaria* that 'in Burke's writings, indeed, the germs of almost all political truths are to be found' (Gandy and Stanlis 1983: xix). And Wordsworth's judgement was even more laudatory: 'Burke was . . . by far the greatest man of his age' (ibid.).[4] Across the Atlantic too Burke enjoyed a favourable early reception. Alexander Hamilton and John Adams were enthusiastic in their compliments (McCue 1997: 16). Macaulay speaks of Burke's 'comprehensive intellect' (ibid.). William Lecky praised Burke's exemplary wisdom (ibid.). Matthew Arnold said that Burke 'saturated politics with thought' (Stanlis 1991: 97). In 1879 John Morley called Burke 'the largest master of civil wisdom in our language' (Gandy and Stanlis 1983: xx). Liberals like Acton and Gladstone admired him as did Conservatives like Disraeli and Lord Hugh Cecil (ibid.). This last observation supplies some obvious initial support for the view that it is proper to see Burke as both a conservative *and* a liberal, a point we will interrogate later. Our list, given the scarcely deniable strength of Burke's reputation, is mostly favourable. The plain fact is that there are more distinguished scholars who admire than oppose him. It is also the case, however, as we will see, that at times the admiration is misconceived. Even so the praise comes from a most distinguished choir of voices across the years.

Summary Praise as Error: Burke as Putative Utilitarian and Positivist

The debate has often seemed, we repeat, in some degree confused. Buckle in his *The History of Civilisation in England,* written between 1857 and 1861, seems to be the first writer to have committed Burke to the ranks of the Utilitarians and positivists. For Buckle, Burke's politics was 'purely empirical' and based on 'general expediency' (Stanlis 1991: 3–4). So convinced of this view was the admiring John Morley, whom we have just seen above endorsing Macaulay's praise, that in the late nineteenth century he praised Burke for his freedom from the 'baneful superstition' that moral thinking has access to a 'supernaturally illumined lamp' for informing the process of political judgement (Morley 1867 in Stanlis 1991: 4).

Morley's contemporaries William Lecky and Leslie Stephen concurred with his utilitarian estimation of Burke. Lecky claimed in 1891 that for Burke church and state were indeed 'based upon expediency' and 'defended by purely utilitarian arguments' (Lecky 1891 in Stanlis 1991: 5). Stephen interpreted Burke in terms of a Utilitarianism derived solely from experience (Stephen 1881: 225–6), a viewpoint which became virtually the British standard for the next eighty years.

There were exceptions in those eighty years. Lewis Namier did not admire Burke's work, but was seemingly more hostile to the company Burke kept with the Rockingham group – which we discussed in Chapter 1 – than to any alleged Utilitarianism. Namier was disposed to see everything, certainly everything eighteenth century, in terms of the factional interest groups to which individuals belonged. For him, Burke was just a Rockingham creature, indeed 'a race-course acquaintance of Rockingham' (O'Brien 1988: xx). This judgement seems blind to Burke's oft-repeated hostility to factionalism.

The standard in America in this period was different: Burke was merely dispatched to virtual oblivion. Russell Kirk points out in his cogent introduction to Peter Stanlis's book that Stanlis himself has been instrumental in restoring Burke's prodigiously high reputation today, alike among conservatives and liberals in the old British sense of the term, both in America and Britain. The fact is that for much of the latter part of the nineteenth century and the first half of the twentieth in the American case, Burke's standing had largely collapsed. Neither the First World War nor the Communist Revolution of 1917 revived it in the United States, says Kirk, but in the aftermath of the Second World War, the gradual dawning on the part of scholars and politicians, as to the nature of totalitarianism, and the human propensity for wayward ideologies, put Burke firmly back in the picture (Kirk 1991).

Burke's reputation as a utilitarian was the most entrenched label history has bestowed on him. Today it is less in evidence. Harold Laski attained perhaps the purest version of the error, when he described Burke as 'a utilitarian who was convinced that what was old was valuable by the mere fact of its arrival at maturity'. Laski thought political philosophy for Burke reduced to 'accurate generalisation from experience' (Laski 1920: 236–7).

Burke has often been seen as a positivist, that is to say concerned with what can be surely and securely identified, measured and recorded. This is an obvious accompaniment to the Utilitarianism alleged. Maurice Cranston said that Burke dismissed natural law and liberty, equality and the rights of man, 'on wholly positivistic grounds'. He was an empiricist with 'a deep, emotional faith in tradition' (The Listener 1957: 100–1). Readers will appreciate that most of these charges of Utilitarianism and positivism come from Burke's admirers. Spoken with admiration or not, they are wrong about the fundamental intellectual orientation of Burkean politics.

Burke and Some General Modern Approbation

It should be stressed, then, that the above claims of Utilitarianism and positivism should not be read as charges against the import of what Burke had to say. At the same time, one is pleased to encounter praise for Burke from less muffled sources. The suggestion of Utilitarianism has the inevitable effect of making Burke sound like a Benthamite. For Burke this would have taken much of the shine off the praise. One suspects that modern scholarship has studied Burke more roundly, than was formerly the case. Certainly, appraisal has now lost its utilitarian emphasis.

Burke would thus certainly have welcomed the very broad encomium of the Catholic historian, Paul Johnson, who calls Burke 'the greatest Irishman who ever lived' (O'Brien 1997).[5]

Robert Grant likewise holds that: 'In some ways Burke is the
greatest of all political thinkers' (Grant 1986). Frank Canavan
calls Burke, 'A profound and luminous mind' (Canavan 1960:
194). Father Canavan also says that for Burke, 'Society was made
by man. But it was made in history under the direction of divine
providence' (ibid.: 191). The two short sentences in this second
observation seem to this author to catch the very essence of
Burke's views.

Burke's Three-Pronged Achievement

Stanlis too accords Burke a shining reception. He identifies
three elements in the achievement. First, there is Burke's conception of society and his appeal to history. Here Stanlis echoes
Lord Acton, who opined that 'History . . . hails from Burke'
(Stanlis 1991: 104). Acton meant that subsequent approaches to
history have in spirit and method been greatly influenced by
Burke. Second, for Stanlis, come Burke's political principles
and approaches in practical politics. Third, Stanlis salutes his
literary genius and superlative prose. Apart from this select trio
of praises, Stanlis stresses, at great length, Burke's vast legal and
historical erudition (Stanlis 1991).[6]

   The Oxford Companion to Philosophy, on the other hand, sounds
a disconcertingly dull note. Professor R.S. Downie says Burke's
writings 'exemplify rhetoric at the expense of reasoned argument'. He also doubts the accuracy of the common view that
Burke was a great orator (Downie 1995: 110). This damning
with no praise at all is against the trend today. The empirical
question of the oratory is worth investigation, although space
does not permit that here.

   We have thus far stuck with our title, showing, without much
detailed substantive discussion, that Burke has received great
acclaim along with some shafts of sharp derision. We must now
proceed to consider some of the commentary on Burke's output
in more depth. The obvious place to begin is with the reception
of his masterpiece. It is surely the most important of his writings.

Space, once again, will not permit us to dwell much on Burke's other work, though we are very mindful of Grant's correct contention that *Reflections* is not a key to the whole corpus. Even so one of this chapter's central questions concerns the reception that successive generations have given Burke's most celebrated book.

From Derision to Resounding Acclaim: *Reflections on the Revolution in France* and Its Ongoing Audience

We can certainly say that *Reflections* has survived better as an account of the nature of British politics than as a causal analysis of the French Revolution, as Hill points out (Hill 1975: 276).[7] It also remains highly plausible, indeed extraordinarily perceptive, as an assessment of the French opening stages of what in the twentieth century was to be called 'totalitarianism'.

Even if its *causal account* of the catastrophe which Burke took the upheaval to be, is inadequate, or lopsided, however, this does not rob the book of all or even most of its value. If Burke was wrong on the causes he was absolutely right on the effects. It is also proper to say that Burke would surely have found the annual French celebration of France's revolution intolerable.

This author cannot get into the French mind either; but confesses to his own difficulty in knowing how the French can widely and annually celebrate a terror-infused insurgency which resulted in the murder of the largely blameless French monarch and his Queen, and of the flower of the French nobility, as well as in ruthless missionary wars against France's neighbours. By way of establishing good totalitarian precedent, moreover, the presiding gangster-ideologues of the movement plundered and persecuted the Catholic Church and set about murdering each other. All this, Burke rightly 'guesstimated', mostly *before* the grisly events themselves. How much more does one need to do to establish one's academic credentials? Burke did not, however, in his early efforts construct the argument in a way likely to promote its success.

The reception accorded to Burke's *Reflections on the Revolution in France* begins, in the event, in an atmosphere, largely of Burke's own making, shifting uncertainly between suspicious unease and puzzlement. In some quarters the reaction was indeed derision and scorn. The story of this initial reception is very neatly related and explained by Mitchell in the fine introduction to his edited version. Mitchell makes it clear that on important as well as trivial empirical details, Burke had been slapdash. It was clearly a serious error on Burke's part to confuse the French tax system with France's local government (Mitchell 1993: viii–ix). His having mistakenly said that Marie Antoinette's bedroom sentinel had been murdered guarding her door (ibid.: ix) might seem today less important substantively, though we can guess that its emotional effect at the time was doubtless strong.

In the event, Mitchell says, the revolution seemed to some English people a kind of tourist attraction. The allegedly murdered sentinel, as it happens, was regaling English visitors with tales of his experience (ibid.: vii–ix). Mitchell says that the educated English public were generally bemused that so universally recognized a scholar as Burke should have left himself open to attack in this way (ibid.: ix). Benjamin Vaughan, who was an eyewitness of the events, decided Burke was just not worth answering, and simply spent an idle two weeks (ibid.).

The French press, on the other hand, merely dismissed the work as bizarre (ibid.). Some critics, however, took the cynical view that Burke had sold out to George III, one of the book's few initial admirers, for the sake of a pension (ibid.). It is certainly undeniable that George was fulsome in his praise of the work: 'A good book, a very good book, and every gentleman should read it' (Kirk 1991: vii). Others took the view that Burke was indeed a crypto-Catholic (ibid.). Certainly, *Reflections* does indeed expend much time and space in defence of the French Catholic Church (ibid.). My personal view on this is that he must inevitably have felt Catholic loyalties all his life. He was a man of solid loyalties. He would surely have believed, however, given his understanding of the impulses behind the Revolution, that this was a threat to *Christian civilization in general*. In this sense the charge of Catholicism made by his critics rather collapses.

Other authorities saw the work as fractured by inconsistency, because Burke had earlier championed other national revolutions, for example in America and Ireland. The very urbane Thomas Jefferson reacted to *Reflections* with the famous lines: 'The Revolution in France does not astonish me as much as the revolution in Mr Burke' (ibid.: viii). One may take it that as events unfolded the kindly Jefferson must have changed his mind. Burke's support for the American colonists indeed makes clear that Burke does not oppose all revolutions. Elliott Barkan rightly says there is no contradiction between Burke's acceptance of and support for the American Revolution and his hostility to the Revolution in France. This distinction involved no hypocrisy, merely a logical extension of his views on the dramatic difference between these events (Barkan 1972: vii).

Mitchell says that some readers took the brutal view that Burke had gone mad. There had been speculation of the sort for some time (ibid.). In a clear reference to Dryden's famous words on the subject in *Absolom and Achitophel*, Mitchell observes that the line of division between genius and insanity was thought to be a thin one (ibid.).[8] Certainly Mitchell does not deny the charge that much of the language of *Reflections* is intemperate. Indeed some of it is violent. Burke's friend Fox, still close though their friendship was later to founder, joked that had Burke been in favour of the Revolution he would have been hanged for it (ibid.: x).

Reflections was also notable, however, as the dire nature of the revolutionary impulsion became swiftly and increasingly evident, for its ability to attract defectors from the camp of opposition, in order to enlist them in the ranks of support. For example, Sir James Mackintosh, in his *Vindiciae Gallicae* (1791), initially disdained Burke's arguments, seeing them as an empty set disguised by brilliant rhetoric. The events of 1792–4 so changed his mind, however, that by the end of the decade he proclaimed that the magnificent rhetoric was actually concealing the force and vigour of the argument (O'Brien 1997: 223–4).

Burke's Essential Concerns in *Reflections*

Burke's masterpiece, however, is not narrow, not a matter of scorn on his part for another nation and the lauding of his own. It is very important to note that in addition to sounding his worries about the French polity and the Catholic Church, *Reflections* also contains in its earlier sections long 'sub-reflections' on the political ups and downs of seventeenth-century England, that clutch of upheavals which Burke saw as having been fortunately resolved by the 'Glorious Revolution' of 1688. One might say that, not in any sense of impertinent scorn, the French are being shown by Burke how in times of political upset and of the pressing and bewildering imperatives of redefinition and clarification of politics, matters of improvement and re-stabilization might best be managed. Burke cares most about his home patch; but he does care about France, both for her own – and great sake – and for the sake of others who may be embroiled with her troubles if she does not surmount them.

Burke sets his face against the artificiality of French planning and administration. Mitchell says Burke scorns the views of Condorcet (Mitchell 1993: xvi). Mitchell may here be adverting to Burke's hostility to the a priori re-planning of French central and regional administration on geometric lines. Though Burke criticizes the Revolution in this as in other respects, he does not actually mention Condorcet anywhere in *Reflections* (Burke 1790).

After Its Uncertain Start,
Reflections Soon Found Favour

Quite early on and on grounds of real substantive weight, many writers concluded favourably with regard to *Reflections*. Concerning the *conceptual* content which Burke discerned to be the essence of the French upheaval, some scholars and other interested parties rapidly acceded to Burke's fundamental excoriation of the events in France on *moral grounds*. If we may adopt modern parlance, the question how the book 'played with' its readership, *is* a crucial one, which is why it is a central concern of this chapter. Whatever hostility it generated at the time and has occasioned at times since, the book, after a wobbly start, established itself as a popular work.

A significant element in the book's wide readership concerned what it said about the respective intellectual and moral character of British and French politics at the time. One might respond to this by saying that, certainly since the seventeenth century, never has English/British political life been suffused with such horror as the contagion which infected France in the 1790s.

Now, however, having set out Burke's views on the form of governance he thought appropriate to human dignity, and having also tried to establish his place in the history of political thought, we must pause defensively. We owe it to his shade to see how he stands up to the brief but damning comments made by the most influential political theorist of the nineteenth and twentieth centuries: Karl Marx, beyond doubt the most influential social theorist of his era. Our elaborate response to the champion of revolution's scornful indictment of the champion of worthwhile tradition will be interwoven with further commentary on Burke's masterpiece. By definition, Burke has nothing direct to say to Marx. For his part Marx had only a few scornful words for Burke. Burke nevertheless represents – in perennial terms – obdurate criticism of everything Marx contends, and the tension between their viewpoints thus rightly dominates this chapter.

On Marx's Hostile Verdict: Burke, Property and the Controversial Bourgeoisie

The founder of Communism's notable *indictment* of Burke in the nineteenth century, we have already mentioned several times.

Marx, adding the claim of 'scientific' demonstration to the 'reason' the French Revolutionaries had thought invincible, labelled Burke a 'bourgeois' spokesman (Marx 1976).[9] How much sense is there to this charge? Frankly, there is very little. Yet replying to it will involve us in some necessary and elaborate argument.

In Burke's day, the word 'bourgeois' had a century before shed its uniquely French character. It had designated in the Middle Ages, a man of seniority, status and property in a French town or city.[10] Bit by bit, subsequently, it became a term for anyone, anywhere, belonging to the shopkeeper or mercantile classes.[11] This group Burke neither belonged to nor spoke for, though he would obviously see their role as vital.

Burke would have been aware both of the original and of the contemporary meaning. In his day, however, 'bourgeois' was not a synonym for 'capitalist'. The latter word existed in principle in English from 1792 (ibid.). But 'capitalism' the noun, that is to say the matrix for the vocabulary so dear to Marx, dates from 1854 (ibid.). It was thus not until after Burke had long been dead that the word 'capitalists' was regularly used to mean the proprietors of the *capitalist* means of industrial production and of large-scale finance.

In truth, eighteenth-century Britain was not 'bourgeois', other than in a preliminary way. Merchants were important, and had been in the past. For example, in the sixteenth century the merchants of Tudor London had shown themselves to be an astonishingly powerful, humane and progressive force (Ramsey 1972). They were a force in the realm, but by no means a 'dominant class'.

It is true that during Burke's lifetime what was subsequently to be called 'capitalism' or the 'market economy', *was* beginning to take shape. Not only was the economy as a whole shifting away from an agrarian, rural-based system, towards an urban, industrial manufacturing one, but agriculture too was becoming transformed, itself being converted into an integral part of the private enterprise system (Ashton 1964). Burke, however, did not know all this.

Nor, moreover, and more significantly for our argument, did his friend Adam Smith. As it happens, exactly the same failure as Burke's to get the measure of the new, emerging bourgeois/capitalist ascendancy applies to Smith, whose ground-breaking theories of the market did *not* include an analysis of the nascent forces of industrial capitalism, nor even an awareness that they were already upon the historical scene. This does not detract from Smith's inspirational genius. He knew better than anyone the marvellous power of markets. He did not know to what heights those powers would be transported by their operating in conjunction with subsequent developments in science and technology. We repeat, however, that neither he nor Burke nor anyone else knew that what we now call the 'Industrial Revolution' was underway.

Burke's lack of understanding of the various new phenomena of industrial and finance capitalism is thus no kind of failure on his part. He was enthusiastic in his support for the idea and reality of 'property', believing as Mitchell says, that it was the institution of property which 'had brought men from the savage to the political state and kept them there' (Mitchell 1993: xviii–xix). His quasi-disciple, Benjamin Constant, waxes even more lyrical in this regard than Burke:

> Without property the human race would be in stasis, in the most brutish and savage state of its existence . . . The abolition of property would destroy the division of labour, the basis of the perfecting of all the arts and sciences. (Constant 2003: 168)

Burke, however, does not like the new moneyed forces. Constant, while still subscribing to the romance of landed wealth, is not hostile to the growing bourgeois forces in society, though he does not call them that (ibid.).[12]

As it happens, and as Grant's very clever paper points out, Burke's one attempt at a kind of economic theorizing, in a little known essay dating from 1795, has the same conceptual apparatus that we associate with Smith. The essay is both *laissez-faire* in assumptions and conclusions and more or less conceives the market in terms of the 'invisible hand'. It does not believe that government can do much about disasters like failed harvests, probably a correct position at the time Burke held it (Burke 1795: 3–7). It is an economic analysis of an agrarian society under the aristocratic mode of governance, as we have called it. It reflects no awareness of the monumental changes occurring in British society at the time and cannot be said, therefore, to be either 'bourgeois' or 'capitalist'.

Marx's charge grates on the historically sensitive ear. Burke could not have seen himself as a member of the *bourgeoisie*. For Marx to call him 'bourgeois' is anachronistic. Burke had little sense of the bourgeoisie, and indeed reveals himself in *Reflections* as hostile to the new moneyed, non-aristocratic interest across the Channel, that is to say the men who were lending to the government and thus acquiring vast powers. Burke points out that 'By the vast debt of France a great moneyed interest had insensibly grown up, and with it a great power' (Burke 1790: 66).

The interesting consideration here is that for Burke to have been the 'bourgeois' lackey that Marx said he was, he would first have had to know that these new moneyed men were the (bourgeois) wave of the future and, second, have been bound accordingly to support them. Neither of these conditions holds. Burke neither supported them nor had any way of knowing that half a century on they would have risen to irresistible political prominence.

The Mechanistic Association of Class with Viewpoint Is False

In any case, we should be wary of mechanistic associations. One of the grosser aspects of Marxism is its reduction of opinion to class interest. The species of argument Marx employs is intrinsically false. Human beings are *not* intellectually reducible to their social origins or current positions. We forget this sometimes, so ferociously have Marxists fought to establish their perverse reductionism. True, Marx's brutal connections often hold if our glance is too casual. In America the rich tend to vote Republican and the less rich Democrat, though with millions of exceptions. It is even clearer that the rich in the British case tend to vote Conservative and the poor to vote Labour. These connections have no logical necessity, however, and break down at key points. Almost all the main movers and shakers in the history of socialism have been bourgeois and some even aristocratic. In the British case a large minority of working-class people have long voted conservative.

The question whether Burke was bourgeois, or an adventurer from the lower Irish gentry or an upwardly mobile hanger-on of the aristocratic mode of governance, is largely irrelevant to a substantive assessment of his intellectual achievements. None of these identifications could ever constitute a sound explanation of Burke's views, let alone of his genius.

Marx sees the bourgeois order as factional, the rule of a special interest, such rule due in time to be replaced by proletarian rule, which will not be factional, since it will comprise the interests of the whole society. We know what a chimera revolutionary socialism has proved to be, resulting, as we shall argue in Chapter 4, in unprecedented factionalism, of blatant vileness. Burke, too, strongly opposed factional government. In his famous *Speech on American Taxation* (1774) he poured scorn on the politics of special interest, despising what he called 'factious and seditious views' (Burke 1774 in Burke 1999: 9).

Burke, Marx and the 'New' Money

In our first two chapters, it was made clear that Burke's policy focus is usually on the *nation*, under what we called 'the aristocratic mode of governance'. Burke did not regard aristocracy, in his broad sense of the term, as factional. In his eyes it governed in the national interest. Actually, Burke would have repudiated anyone whom he suspected of reaching his political opinions merely by intellectualizing his class-interests, so far did he stand from the politics of faction. The aristocratic political mode was not for him a system of exploitation in any sense of the poor being wantonly repressed and subordinated.

Eighteenth-century Britain was the richest country the world had ever seen. By the standards of Western modernity, however, it was still wretchedly poor. Burke did not know about the fabulous wealth that awaited his countrymen in the not too distant future. He could not imagine the immense flow of production necessary to generate that wealth, nor dream of a society where most people are middle class, where even most working-class people have decent housing, and own telephones, cars and so on, possessions of a kind he could know nothing about, of course. The country cared for its poor as best it could. Burke thought the best way to administer the distribution of incomes was to leave it to supply and demand. For example, to attempt in times of distress to help stricken groups by interventions and subsidies, was, precisely, factionalism (Burke 1795: 7). Once again, he was echoed faithfully in this by his admirer Benjamin Constant (Constant 2003).[13]

Burke Knows That Future History Is Mostly Unknowable

Burke knew, of course, that it is our condition not to know what lies in store. Unlike Marx, Burke, despite the formidable rigour of his thinking, and despite his uncanny knack for prediction, did not claim a direct line of insight into the future, nor base his predictions on any supposed 'science' of historical development. Like the great Max Weber, a hundred years later, Burke did not believe the future to be susceptible to much accurate forecasting,[14] though his chancing his arm at prediction in *Reflections* proved astonishingly on target.

Marx could have introduced an element of accuracy into his sneer had he called Burke a creature of the aristocracy. The charge would still be essentially false, because Burke was nobody's 'creature' but rather his own man entirely. What picture might Marx have formed from an honest reading of *Reflections*, that being the obvious place to start? We might accede to Marx's identification of the new moneyed interest in France or Britain as 'bourgeois' or 'capitalist'. Why see Burke as their creature, though? He is for the landed interest, for the Church, for the monarchy and *against* the new money.

Marx, Burke and the 'New' Money Continued

Obviously among the moneyed people who had lent to the French Crown, often speculatively, people who would clearly want their money back, there must have been what Marx and we too would call 'bourgeois' elements. When the state is short of funds and borrows from the rich, obviously those who lend want a return on their money, as well as having a profound and natural interest in recouping their loans. The state services its debts, and repays its loans, often, indeed usually, by way of taxes levied by the government on the ordinary population. In modern societies, since the later decades of the twentieth century, anyway, this burden falls mainly on the employed middle classes, who predominate, by force of numbers, in their share of National Income.

In a pre-modern economy, where the middle class and bourgeois (capitalist) elements are far less in evidence or only embryonic, this fiscal weight falls on the ordinary poor, who are much the biggest group in society. In late eighteenth-century France, says Burke, the intractable fiscal realities of the time inflamed the opinions held of the new rich by many people in the lower orders (Burke 1790: 61–6). And why should they not? It was on the poor majority that the burden of France's financial debt fell most cripplingly.

Burke recognized that British society was much calmer and its finances more orderly than those of the French, but he did detect signs, as we noted in Chapter 1, of radical clergymen, who, not unlike the fanatical French pastor, Rabaut de Saint-Etienne, with his frightful proposal that France destroy everything and begin anew, were ready to raise the radical standard in England. In Chapter 2 we mentioned in this respect, the Revd. Dr Richard Price, whose sermons, according to Burke, so adulated the antinomian tendencies apparent in France.[15] What worried Burke specifically is that the other potential villains of the piece, progressive philosophers like Jeremy Bentham and down at heel aristocrats, desperately in need of money, like Lord Lansdowne, were also present in England, and indeed that groups of such outlook were accustomed to enjoy Lansdowne's hospitality at Bowood, in Wiltshire (Burke 1790 in Mitchell 1993: xiii). Some of the conditions and some of the thinking, that had suborned and subverted France, were present in England too.

The Facts of the Situation Justified Burke's Fears

Given the British government's need to borrow for military and naval purposes, there was a similar need in England to finance the National Debt in the only way really possible, by the country's resorting, as France resorted, to indirect taxation for the financing of loans from wealthy groups and individuals. T.S. Ashton points out that the British National Debt in the eighteenth century was almost entirely driven by war finance (Ashton 1964: 8). Now, the indirect taxation which financed wars was indeed intrinsically 'regressive', which is to say, as we have already noted of the contemporary French context, that poorer groups contributed disproportionately to the revenue raised. This regressive fiscal pattern seems, we repeat, to have caused great resentment in France, where the public finances were in a vastly more chaotic state than was the case with British arrangements.

The French Pillaging of the Church

What profoundly disturbed Burke was the casualness of the French attitude to ownership. The Revolutionaries denied that the holdings of the Church were the same kind of property as property owned by individuals. Burke thought this was sophistry. To attack any property was to attack all property (Burke 1790 in Mitchell 1993: viii). And, to extrapolate from Burke's French musings, if there did indeed exist in England forces comparable to the antinomians in France, might there not be an attack on the institution of property in England, too?

Burke is, then, upholding property, but in no sense is his general stance in *Reflections* compatible with the charge that he represents the new forces of capitalism. He seeks to defend what we have called the aristocratic mode of governance, a system Burke saw as working in the interest of the nation as a whole.

Burke Is Simply Wrong about the New Wealth

Anachronistic Marx's vocabulary may be when it is applied to Burke. Everybody makes errors, however, and in a very different way Burke was wrong too. The new social stratum, the 'moneyed interest', was not in its essence a money-grubbing class, as Burke thought, though doubtless it had many people in its membership who fitted that description. There are plenty of rich 'spivs' in Britain today, and plenty of financial shysters in America.[16] Why should we take them as representative of their overall class? The overall assessment called for of these emerging 'bourgeois' forces is surely very favourable. With the expansion of this class from the nineteenth century onwards, in Britain and America, we witness the most liberating economic trajectory of human betterment the world has ever known. Readers should consider those societies where there is no serious and responsible private enterprise.

Nor can the economic preponderance of the capitalists, where they are the dominant force, be regarded as factional.

The capitalists, the bourgeoisie of modernity, are probably the only rich class in history not in various respects detested by those poorer than they. This is arguably because the middle-class majority and, indeed, most of the working class, have twigged that the free enterprise system, in terms of the living standards achieved, is in the majority interest.

In time Burke would have worked out a systemic understanding of the bourgeois forces. Had he lived at the same time as Marx it is hardly conceivable that his account of the new socio-economic phenomena would have been so distorted and dangerous as Marx's was. Certainly in his one foray into economic analysis, Burke does show a realization that it is precisely the *systemic* aspects of an economy based on property which defends the participants in that system. In the case of the agrarian economy Burke has in mind, the property is mostly aristocratic in Burke's broad sense of the term. Individuals in the aristocracy may be corrupt, but the system in principle militates against corruption. Even the greatest beneficiaries of the system risk losing out if anyone acts irresponsibly with regard to property. To experiment as carelessly as the French revolutionary forces were doing, with a vast swathe of property like that of the Catholic Church, indeed to plunder and even destroy it, seemed the height of folly and immorality to Burke.

The Systemic Controls under the Market Economy Are Stronger than under the Aristocratic Mode of Governance

The systemic controls are stronger, as we now know, in the case of the free enterprise industrial economy of which Burke and Smith were as yet unaware, though it was springing up under their feet. Of course, just as some landed proprietors may be corrupt, so may some businessmen. While there are brakes on corruption under the aristocratic mode of governance, when a market economy grows to a higher level, as was to prove dramatically the British case in the nineteenth century, the brakes on corruption increase proportionately with the immensely more pervasive circulation of economic information. It must be stressed again that we cannot complain that Burke did not know about the cornucopian possibilities of modern free enterprise. It is the case, of course, that he did not. He was a prisoner of his time and if his friend Adam Smith did not know about all this, we can hardly indict Burke for being in the dark about it too. We know even so that Burke has the essential mark of the great scholar of humanity: he goes with the evidence. We may be sure that had he lived in a later time he would have gone with it. It will indeed be argued in Chapter 4 that he would have seen in the colossal economic achievements of the Anglosphere today, an unanswerable vindication of the role of the English-speaking bourgeoisie in human welfare.

Bourgeois as a Sneer Term

The most significant thing about the epithet 'bourgeois' itself was that under Marx's guidance, for about a century and a half, it served as the standard sneering indictment of those who fell in any way foul of the Marxist prospectus. Marx's contemporary, the anarchist philosopher Bakunin, levelled exactly the same charge against Marx (Eastman 1955 in Gottfried 1986: 20). In our day the term 'bourgeois' has now lost much of its force, because it has converged into an almost common meaning with the term 'middle class'. Most of the not very impressive people, who would perhaps like to use the term today, belong to a segment – predominantly the socialist-minded public sector intellectuals – of the broader class it now designates.

Some middle-class people and some working-class ones too, are dishonest financially. The market system would not work if they constituted a majority. Some middle-class people have been infected with antinomian views. They are not a majority but some of them are powerful in their publicly financed redoubts, and their power and beliefs explain much about what is wrong with, for example, our contemporary education systems in America and Britain. This theme and other closely connected ones will be developed in Chapter 4.

Burke versus Plato and Rousseau on the Worth of Human Beings

In its ability to attract and repel alike, in terms of a large and influential audience, in its day and in subsequent times, *Reflections* surely bears at least some mild comparison with Plato's *Republic*. It is Burke's masterpiece, as it happens, which has the better favourable/unfavourable ratio of response. Many readers, furthermore, will surely find Burke much the more likable intellectual Guardian of the two.[17]

Plato's *Republic*, in its ultra-rationalism, its first principles approach to politics, is a clear ancestor of what the French revolutionaries were trying to create in Burke's day. It is no surprise to find that Rousseau much admired Plato's work. Indeed he believed that Plato's *Republic* was the best treatise on education ever written (Rousseau 1762). In Plato, as in Rousseau, the ideas of politics and education are solidly entwined, a significant and menacing embrace we will comment on in Chapter 4.

Plato proposes an austere and philistine republic run by 'Guardians', men and women of pure character, who will organize the lives of less intelligent folk on wholesome lines. They are even empowered to lie to these lesser souls, systematically, on prudential grounds. About the only agreement between *Reflections* and *The Republic* is their authors' common belief in leadership. For Burke, however, leadership emerges with the organically rooted development of a society. For Plato, as for Rousseau, the brilliant, on the basis of their rational contemplation of things, have the right and duty to decide what is what for their fellows. Their leadership, like the system they lead, is plucked from an a priori sky. The governance proposed by Plato is *indecent*, as Karl Popper rightly alleged (Popper 1965). So was the governance of Revolutionary France. Artificial societies, based on lies or unusable abstractions, will always fail.

Burke as Innovator

Many of Burke's admirers have lauded him as an innovator. This is especially true of his work on the Revolution in France. This is one of the great critiques of revolutionary ideology and politics. One might want to ask how well it shapes up alongside the twentieth-century critiques of totalitarianism: Koestler, Orwell, Popper, Hayek and Kolakowski.[18] In fact the French Revolution supplied later manifestations of the totalitarian *zeitgeist* with a model very easy for sharp, intolerant minds to imitate. My inclination in response would be to regard Burke's masterpiece as *the* template for the study of modern despotism. His work is at least as great as any of these later masterworks, and more groundbreaking. Consider this extract from Burke's *Second Letter on a Regicide Peace* (1796*b*), drawn to our attention by O'Brien (O'Brien 1997: 319–20):

> It is a dreadful truth, but it is a truth that cannot be concealed; in ability, in dexterity, in the distinctness of their views, the Jacobins are our superiors. They saw the thing right from the very beginning. Whatever were the first motives to the war among politicians, they saw that it is in its spirit, and for its objects, a *civil war;* and as such they pursued it. It is a war between the partisans of the ancient, civil, moral, and political order of Europe against a sect of fanatical and ambitious atheists which means to change them all. It is not France extending a foreign empire over other nations: it is a sect aiming at universal empire, and beginning with the conquest of France. (Burke 1796*b*: 3)

This is of course an eighteenth-century observation. Notice, however, that there is nothing in this extract except the noun 'France' to stop its being a twentieth-century reference. If we were talking about the twentieth century, 'France' in the last sentence could be substituted by either 'Russia' or 'Germany', without any loss of meaning for the spirit of the paragraph as a whole, nor for any of its chilling details.

The French Revolution created a new kind of societal type, the totalitarian society. The French Revolutionaries conquered France and then set out to conquer Europe. The Communists and Nazis, more ambitious and good learners, respectively subverted Russia and Germany as a prelude to the ambition of world conquest. European totalitarianism involved the subversion of great societies, actual (France and Germany) and potential (Russia). Burke's articulation of this new phenomenon is an insight of genius. He had only the one exemplar, but he spotted its novel and anomalous character.

A Note on *Thoughts on the Cause of the Present Discontents* (1770)

One is mindful of Grant's insistence that *Reflections* does not encompass the whole of Burke's genius, although it is the book posterity will most celebrate as long as there are free societies and English remains so successful a medium. Burke *does* focus on despotism, but he is far from wholly absorbed by such corruption. He also contributed vital insights into the governance of free societies.

In the heyday of Victorian politics, Burke's pamphlet *Thoughts on the Cause of the Present Discontents* was interpreted not only as the defence of the Rockingham Whigs that it clearly was, but also, according to B.W. Hill, as a blueprint for the two-party system of modernity. Hill says that though Burke does not explicitly support alternations in government and the reduction of the political power of the crown, there is some justification for this subsequent Victorian view taken of our author (Hill 1975: 16–17). These constitutional issues, and others of social organization, remain vital to Burke as we shall see in Chapter 4.

Other Burkean Issues

There are many other themes in relation to Burke and questions about the man which should be touched on. Most can be left to Chapter 4, which seeks to establish Burke's relevance today. We will, however, consider a few of them here.

Burke and prejudice

Burke thought the age in which he lived was less enlightened than its mostly self-appointed pundits assumed. For this reason, he took one of the central concepts of the vocabulary of Enlightenment, namely the word 'prejudice' as pejoratively understood, and raised it on a flag of contempt for the age's complacency. For Burke prejudice was reason, not individual but *social* reason, encased in sentiment and habit and transmitted from age to age in the only form in which it could be transmitted, as prepossession and bias of the mind and affections. This collective reason is under the guidance of the Divine Reason. This does not mean men must accept all prejudices. It does mean that they must take them seriously (Canavan 1960: 78–9).

He never seems to have attempted consistency in his use of the word, in fact, as any persistent reading of his intellectual output will show. Unsurprisingly he used 'prejudice' in its (then as today) contemporary, conventional sense of 'benighted', 'bigoted' and so on *before* his assertion of 'prejudice' as signifying approbation. More interesting is his decision to continue employing the contemporary, standard meaning of the word *after* he had begun using it favourably.

H.B. Acton remarks – so Francis Canavan points out – how striking was Burke's choosing to defend tradition, under the name of prejudice. Obviously this was in defiance of his own age (ibid.: 74). As Canavan remarks, 'The eighteenth century, which regarded itself peculiarly as an Age of Reason, was wont to distinguish the reason it adored from the prejudice it abhorred' (ibid.: 73).

The Burke innovation seems to have stuck. At least conservatives still often use 'prejudice' in defiance of current nonsense
and it seems likely that the usage does come down to us from
Burke. It is possible that a prejudice might revive around the
idea of 'empire', for example, as it once was in the old, proud
sense of 'Empire Day', as celebrated in the days before the
British had lost their political confidence. Or one might claim
to have a prejudice in favour of marriage rather than unmarried
cohabitation.

Burke, providence and prudence

As the last chapter and the present have stressed, Burke holds
to the notion of divine providence. Burke's moral views are
ultimately bound up with this. It evidently did not deter Gibbon
in his admiration. We cannot, should not, overlook the fact,
however, that for some notable scholars the notion of a divine
providence is quite unacceptable. Professor John Gray, for
example, has observed that it is precisely on the grounds of
Burke's providentialism, the notion that God has arranged for
the historical process to permit our redemption, that he feels
most impelled to reject him.[19]

Gray rejects the notion of Divine Providence, on principle.
I return, though, to the view that Burke's political positions, at
the level of practice, are consistent with most religious opinions
or none at all. As Grant points out, not only is Burke well-
disposed to Christianity in general; he is also well-disposed to
Hinduism (Grant 1986: 9). None of my concessions amounts
to a rejection of the Burkean position, however.

Providence is for Burke the support God gives to man in
respect of man's having been created free. Burke believed that
the hope and fear which mark our humanity would have no
object to reverence if fatality were our human lot. Men cannot
live under the assumption of what today is called determinism.
Burke believed that the science and mathematical advances of

the seventeenth century led precisely to a fatalistic view of reality (Canavan 1960: 30–2). Human nature as willed by the Deity is the proper source of our moral philosophy. The collective reason of the human race is under the guidance of Divine wisdom (ibid.: 78).

The two key features of the doctrine of Providence are that men are truly free and that there is an ineluctable guidance of our pathways by the Creator. We noted in Chapter 2 that Professor Canavan says that reconciling these two elements is a profound problem in metaphysics and theology, but Burke did not struggle with it and neither need we (ibid.: 178). Our political prudence, in the face of the uncertainty we endlessly encounter, consists in our acting mainly on the basis of what we know *ordinarily* happens. Prudence does not yield perfectly certain results, but it leads to the best approximations. The rules of prudence are given 'by the known march of the ordinary providence of God' (ibid.: 14).

Burke on religion and, one hopes, the faltering charge of Utilitarianism

By now it has been made abundantly clear that in order to charge Burke with Utilitarianism, scholars must suppress or simply forget the fact, which Burke's words often reinforce if we search them out, that he was a Christian, who believed the world had been created by a loving, Divine being, a God who has set us clear moral instructions. Very sophisticated writings, notably those of Stanlis and Canavan have sought to establish precisely this. Those who label Burke a Utilitarian are simply choosing not to recognize that he sees man as under Divine guidance.

In Chapter 2 it was readily conceded that Burke took usefulness as an important practical and moral category. We have reasserted that truth in this chapter too. In the moral order, however, usefulness cannot take pride of place. As Constant was to point out about a decade after Burke's death, I will derive much more comfort from a man's believing he has no right to kill me without due cause, than in his not finding it *useful* to expedite my decease (Constant 2004: 41).

That said, we should not lose sight of the truth that day to day we do, all of us, live with what is practical, useful and traditional, what seems to work. This subjection of ours, unites both those who believe there is no other standard than the utilitarian and those who believe that there are higher standards we must obey, but that much of the time we can engage ourselves with what is practical and useful. It is probably best to say that Burke was a Utilitarian, *secondarily*, which meant most of the time when his *primary* beliefs were not asked for.

That the issue is not cut and dried is, we have admitted, in part Burke's own fault. The endlessly repeated charges of Utilitarianism levelled against Burke are a function of Burke's repeated utilitarian vocabulary, which simply occludes the matter. It has countless times been said that his opinions were based, ultimately, on what he thought most generally *useful, practical and habitual*, on what time and experience had shown, in his view, to *function most usefully and effectively for most people*.

On some reasonable reckonings the charge is true. Most certainly Burke treasures the long-lasting, the practical and the useful. He says so, again and again. There are, however, separate grounds, more basic ones, transcendental ones in fact, on which he treasures them *ultimately*. Burke to some extent talks himself into a corner by his so overwhelmingly choosing to speak the language of practicalities. His deeper beliefs, however, *are* available to scrutiny. The corpus of his work is enormous. It seems that some of his friends, as much as his foes, have not read enough of it.

Burke has left this impression of being wedded merely or at least mostly to time-hallowed usefulness, scattered widely and repeatedly in his writings and speeches. Such Utilitarianism was the apparent drift of his observations and arguments. It is perhaps because he was not in the formal sense an academic philosopher, and because he was so contemptuous of superficial and pre-emptive claims to human rights in the abstract, that he did not take sufficient care to stress his belief in the God-given rights and wrongs of the human race.

Why Did Burke Not Make His Ultimate Views More Clear?

The claim that Burke is at core a Utilitarian is held by supporters and opponents alike. A number of very famous names have subscribed to it. Some strong enthusiasts for Burke, on the other hand, regard the claim as so false as to verge on intellectual calumny. The very existence of the controversy suggests that Burke may have *chosen* not to make his ultimate beliefs crystal clear. The decision to hold back from posterity unambiguously explicit information is actually a puzzling habit among many of the historically great. We know that Shakespeare was a conservative. We know he perceived mystery at the core of the human condition. What else do we know, for sure, about his deepest views?

The case is somewhat similar with Burke, though nothing like so obscure, given that political writing is usually more explicitly opinion-laden than poetry. If Burke's views were more explicit, more transparent, then perhaps there would be less reason to burrow into in his work. Perhaps, though, there is no such thing as unambiguous clarity in intellectual greatness, at least when it comes to political commentary, the variety of human circumstance being so rich and various that no political writer can seem consistent as he deals with it. Burke's readers were certainly surprised that he seemed to countenance revolutions in some places – in late seventeenth-century England, and late eighteenth-century America – but not in late eighteenth-century France. Burke's distinctions here may reflect what he considered useful to do, but they can also be justified by the differences of moral context, a point which Barkan makes very emphatically (Barkan 1972: vii).

Burke: Liberal or Conservative?

Another substantive issue, however, concerns questions of Burke's fundamental political orientation. In 1930 Sir Lewis Namier rather frostily proclaimed that since the Rockinghams, to whose version of Whig politics Burke subscribed – indeed he did so in his capacity as their principal apologist – were both authoritarian and conservative, Burke too must be seen as essentially a conservative (Namier 1961 in Hill 1975: 63). This reception of a very complex writer, this decision to buttonhole him, seems crude today. In fact it is not obvious why Namier should have wanted to frame the question in terms demanding so black and white an answer. Why should Burke not be both a liberal and a conservative? The notion that a person must be one or the other is quite unnecessarily confining and constricting.

Was not Oakeshott both a liberal and a conservative? Was not Churchill? Was not Milton Friedman? Is not Thatcher? These are all people who believed – like Burke – in their country and its history and achievements. They all believed in individual freedom and responsibility. They all distrusted vast plans constructed by 'experts' for the 'salvation' of others, recognizing that 'damnation' would be a better term for what such unfortunates have usually been subjected to.

Grant and Oakeshott on Burke and Associations

Men live individually and socially. Their individuality is socially formed, but constitutes a marvellous feature of the human *differentia specifica*, with its immense range of personal differentiation. Grant says that Burke is the first great modern critic of what his intellectual descendant Michael Oakeshott calls 'rationalism in politics' (Grant 1986). This latter is the Cartesian, hubristic philosophy, which, as if there were no yesterdays, sees current inhabitants of the world as fruitfully employed when they engage, on the contrary, in isolated, atomistic contemplation of our human lot, without a jot of historical sense or hint of indebtedness. Indeed, they have a habit of dismissing all experience in favour of their own present thought. This is an ancient error, going back via Rousseau to Plato, which we discuss briefly again in Chapter 4.

According to Grant, Oakeshott says that Burke thought of associations in contractual, individualist terms (ibid.). You look at the Boy Scouts or the Samaritans and you join or do not, on private and un-coerced grounds. Grant concedes this of many associations – one voluntarily decides to become a doctor or lawyer and does, or does not, succeed in this. Grant insists, however, that personal choice is not true of the most permanent ones – family and country. Here, Burke explicitly says, we have no choice, either as to our membership, or as to the 'natural' duties it entails. And he spoke also of a society where such obligations had lapsed, as prone to dissolve into 'the dust and powder of individuality' (Burke in Grant 1986).

Burke might, one is sad to confess, be speaking precisely of our own society. If we seek greater social coherence, there will need to be a sufficient number of key thinkers, supporters of a moral *status quo ante*, to achieve minimal critical momentum in a restorative political orientation. When country, family, patriotism and national history are neglected and repudiated, and many of our associations are becoming unstuck, we are surely threatened with social disintegration and chaos.

Burke on the Good and the Bad and the Ordinary

There is another consideration, however, in relation to this bewitching English/Irishman, which Burke's readers may have absorbed unconsciously. Certainly one does not find it explicitly articulated in the literature. Perhaps this author should more honestly say he has not precisely found it anywhere in Burke's writings, merely *sensed* it, everywhere in them. The point is that

Reflections is notable, perhaps even above all, for its genial moral reckoning of humankind. *Reflections*, like all Burke's work really, has an optimistic view of ordinary human potential. This is for me Burke's invisible writing. It is somewhere there, repeatedly, between the lines. One of the great fallacies, taught to generations of Politics undergraduates, is that conservatism is pessimistic and socialism, for example, optimistic. This contention is regarded, even by those who believe it, as a cliché. In fact it is not even a cliché; it is simply not true. People like Burke, and his modern disciple Oakeshott, believe that if a society is decently governed its members will also mostly be decently behaved. Of course for conservatives like Burke, 'decently governed' means 'decently governed in time-proven ways'. Socialist 'optimism' means abandoning tested experience in favour of a lot of heady plans which do not work out and drifting abstractions which can never be put into proper operation given their elusive properties.

Before we draw this chapter to a close, however, we must deal with one more catchword of the Enlightenment's thinking: the so-called 'sensibility'.

Burke and Rousseau's Sensibility

The French Enlightenment did not generate only a new politics, with the disastrous results, many still with us, we have outlined in this and the first two chapters. The same pattern of a-historical and rootless a priori speculation was extended to the realm of philosophical psychology. Along with the new politics there came a new concept of personhood, a self-caressing egotism which despite its lack of historical substance has had a lasting impact on European literature. At the centre of it stood the bewildering, brilliant and destructive figure of Rousseau. Stanlis defines sensibility as 'a moral and aesthetic theory based upon sentiment, with important ramifications in politics and society' (Stanlis 1991: 159). Sensibility had a massive impact on English literature too (ibid.: 159–62).

Rousseau was the main prophet and exemplar of sensibility (ibid.: 163). Stanlis even makes the astounding claim that Rousseau was instrumental in infusing the abstracted rationalism of the Enlightenment,.with this new idea which merged into it, even becoming the predominant element, such that the Cartesian logic which proclaimed 'cogito ergo sum' (I am thinking, therefore I exist) was in part eclipsed by 'je sens, donc je suis' (I am feeling, therefore I exist) (ibid.).

The greatest English writers – Swift, Fielding, Johnson and Burke – were all humanists and Christians and resistant both to the abstract cogitation and the self-flattering cultivation of feelings, regarding their combination as a pagan hedonism (ibid.: 162). To get some flavour of the dangers 'sensibility' involved, consider these sentences by Mary Wollstonecraft, in her autobiographical novel, *Mary*:

Softened by tenderness the soul is disposed to be virtuous. Is any sensual gratification to be compared to that of feeling the eyes moistened after having comforted the unfortunate?

Wollstonecraft's grammar is not too good in the second, longer sentence. It is presumably her person rather than just her eyes which have done the comforting. In any case, the appalling, pharisaical self-regard and vulgar pride displayed – the woman is weeping with joy at the thought of her own virtue – would surely deter most readers.

Sad to say, however, as the rest of Stanlis's fine chapter 5 makes clear, there were no signs of Rousseau's influence in France abating at any time in the late eighteenth century. Among twentieth-century French Gurus the cult of sensibility was alive and kicking. Jean-Paul Sartre's vanity rivalled that of Rousseau. As it happens, Burke knew Rousseau and was witness to his Olympian vanity and furious self-regard. For details, I recommend Stanlis's chapter 5 as worth careful study.

This chapter has, its author hopes, sketched out a fairly detailed initial assessment of the reception given to Burke's thinking. Let us close by citing the words of the greatest

Englishman of the twentieth century on a writer whom Paul
Johnson calls 'the greatest Irishman who ever lived'.

Churchill on Burke

We have meandered across a wide range of the receptions
given to Burke by his contemporaries and the scholars who
have succeeded him. Some have been uninhibitedly favourable
and well-conceived. Others have applauded him but missed
crucial parts of his message. Others, fewer in number, have
excoriated him as the servile creature of dominant interests.
Nothing could honour him more than Churchill's masterly
praise:

> On the one hand [Burke] is revealed as a foremost apostle of
> Liberty, on the other as the redoubtable champion of Author-
> ity. But a charge of political inconsistency applied to this life
> appears a mean and petty thing. History easily discerns the
> reasons and forces which actuated him, and the immense
> changes in the problems he was facing which evoked from
> the same profound mind and sincere spirit these entirely
> contrary manifestations. His soul revolted against tyranny,
> whether it appeared in the aspect of a domineering Monarch
> and a corrupt Court and Parliamentary system, or whether,
> mouthing the watch-words of a non-existent liberty, it towered
> up against him in the dictation of a brutal mob and wicked
> sect. No one can read the Burke of Liberty and the Burke
> of Authority without feeling that here was the same man
> pursuing the same ends, seeking the same ideals of society
> and Government, and defending them from assaults, now
> from one extreme, now from the other. (Winston Churchill
> *Consistency in Politics*[20])

4

Under Burkean Eyes: Burke and Our
Present Blessings and Woes

What Can Burke Tell Us Today?

This chapter will contend that Burke's relevance for civilized societies is as great today as ever. McCue's persuasive book exemplifies the perennial range and pertinence of Burke's thinking (McCue 1997). There is still no better guide than he to civilization and its governance. Burke is a Renaissance man, an *uomo universale*, rivalling Sam Johnson in breadth of knowledge. He is also perhaps a man of the Enlightenment, but in the same cautious spirit as his friend Adam Smith. Burke is 'enlightened' rather than 'Enlightened', being mostly hostile to the French philosophers of his day. Indeed, Burke deserves pride of place among their opponents.

The Advanced English-Speaking
Societies and Their Conceits

Frank Canavan observes that actually 'Burke thought the age in which he lived was less enlightened than its mostly self-appointed pundits assumed'. Fearing that our present conceits have already had certain appalling results and that these could grow worse, I suggest that the charge of over-generous self-estimation on the part of the English-speaking world may fit the present age as well as it did the late eighteenth century. Indeed, it is in some ways even more true today, a proposition which we must explore, with the help of Burkean concepts, a 'Burkean prism' so to speak.

Burke's Priceless Common Sense Fortifies His Intellectual Brilliance

Burke's supreme value lies in his everyday wisdom; his clear, feet-on-the-ground, reasonableness. This unshakeable common sense contributes as much as his erudition to his fundamental achievement – his critique of abstract rationalism. In Burke the ancient virtue of common sense is raised to heights unequalled by any thinker of his time or since. Chesterton's telling phrase 'the starry pinnacle of the commonplace' applies, ironically, much more to Burke's achievement than his own. This is not just because Burke surpassed him intellectually. It is also because Burke shared none of Chesterton's factional bigotry in religion and politics. Burke raised up decent commonplaces in the Christian spirit which commends the raising up of Samaritans and publicans. And Burke was the enemy extraordinary of factionalism.

His grasp of the commonplace comes into its own when he is dealing with wayward, outlandish things. Perhaps the unerring eye for the normal and healthy equipped him for recognizing pathology when he saw it. In any event, Burke was peculiarly suited to dealing with a phenomenon such as the French Revolution, even when its infancy meant that full empirical exemplars (developed instances in the real world) were not available.

Burke Prefers Simplicity and Economy in Argument

Because of *Reflections*, Burke is famous above all for his analysis of those dogmatic convulsions we now classify as wayward ideologies. Mostly, however, his focus is an everyday one. He prefers the Occam's Razor convention for explanation, that is doing it simply, with minimum intellectual apparatus. He holds that everything is what it is and not some other thing. He likes quotidian explanation for quotidian things. When he has to stand outside everyday things, as in *Reflections* or in *Letters on a Regicide Peace*, he naturally engages a different imaginative gear and produces far from everyday conclusions.

Burke's Assessment of the Revolution in France Was Correct

For his own day the almost immediate outcomes of the Revolution in France show how justified Burke's hostility was. We noted in chapters 2 and 3 his grasp of its long-term potential too. His criticism of the French Revolution really amounts to the first systematic critique of what twentieth-century scholars were to call 'totalitarianism'.

Fortunately, we may say of Napoleon, that for all his cynical ruthlessness, although he had been a beneficiary, he was not a *partisan* of the deranged mode of revolutionary governance which after Waterloo, having been abandoned by him, dropped out of application for the rest of the nineteenth century. This was no more than a lull on the part of the incubus in question. In the twentieth century it proved a gross human misfortune that the Marxists had kept the debate alive on the theoretical front during this quiescence, indeed had much enlarged the revolutionary claims, adding the title 'science' to the 'reason' which the French had claimed as the metaphysic of the exercise. From the conservative or classical liberal viewpoint, the ideas and institutions emerging from France's revolutionary convulsions may be said to have haunted and corrupted the human imagination ever since.

Most modern opponents of totalitarianism will concur with Burke's judgement on French developments in his day. In twentieth-century totalitarianism, his larger fears are fully vindicated. The first issue of the new British monthly, *Standpoint*, features a compelling discussion of Stalin and Mao and the dizzying scale of their wickedness. The picture is of rampant, unconstrained power, bent solely on its own exercise (Chang and Montefiore 2008). We may surely see Mao, in particular, as a Chinese Rabaud de St Etienne on a gigantic scale. Rabaud was the Protestant pastor who featured in Chapter 2, calling for the total destruction of French society.

Factionalism, Totalitarianism and the Free Society

Burke was utterly opposed to the dominance of factious outlooks in politics. Selfish British interest groups had prevented the economic advance of Ireland. The break with America may seem inevitable to us now but Burke believed obstinate British factionalism had been at the core of the dispute, while ruthless intrigue by the East India Company had produced the British disgrace in India under Warren Hastings. Burke's words in *Reflections* leave us, moreover, in no doubt as to the factionalism which drives the Revolution in France:

> The resources of intrigue are called in to supply the defects of argument and wit. To this system of literary monopoly[1] was joined an unremitting industry to blacken and discredit in every way, and by every means, all those who did not hold to their faction. To those who have observed the spirit of their conduct, it has long been clear that nothing was wanted but the power of carrying the intolerance of the tongue and of the pen into a persecution which would strike at property, liberty, and life. (Burke 1790: 68)

The tale has since become more gruesome by far. Nazism induced the whole German nation to undertake a factional war against the world. Communism was, everywhere, a factional war waged *against* whole peoples, in the Soviet case, many nations, by Marxist elites. How many people, today, know that under

Communism, the senior party members enjoyed an entirely separate medical dispensation? How many know that in many Communist countries certain goods could be bought only with hard currency, a status no Communist money ever achieved? This was the institutionalization of economic mediocrity and kow-towing to a cosseted faction. For many years in the twentieth century, a third of the world's population was ruled by Marxist special interests, by remote bureaucratic and ideological factions with no concerns for the general welfare. The results included wretched poverty, vicious persecution of dissent, and murder on a scale unimaginable to previous generations.

Burke had the *essential* measure of this new despotism, mostly *avant la lettre*, though in the event the evil he excoriated was far exceeded by later versions. Some of the habits of Communism live on in the countries which endured this intellectualized slavery. At least, however, their populations today know that the experience has left a ruinous legacy, most notably, as travellers to the former Communist lands know, in the form of a terrible distrust between individuals. When, in Burke's words, 'The State is all-in-all' (Burke 1796*a*: 16), then even when the system collapses, the poisoned moral order takes years to recover.

Among anti-totalitarian writings, Burke's *Reflections* and his *Letters on a Regicide Peace*, warrant pride of place for imaginative insight, though modern transport and technology have meant that the scale of wickedness would probably have surprised even Burke himself. Moreover, the factionalism he so detested, has since entrenched itself on a huge scale in the modern free societies, as we shall see shortly. In unfree societies factionalism is the rule, since their governance is always in the service of special interest. The ruling faction is that part which dominates the whole. Such was always the case in the totalitarian societies.

This utterly falsified the Marxist claim that a socialized economy would liberate mankind. Instead it facilitated the predatory rent-seeking of the controlling faction. This is also the common, though not the universal, case in Islamic societies. Nor is faction a question of mere numbers. Factions by definition circumscribe, even suppress or try to, interests other than their own. *Apartheid* South Africa was factional in the service of the white minority. Post-*Apartheid* South Africa has many factions, but the most significant is that of the black *majority*, at least in its window-dressing and propping up of smaller black factions. Neither is factionalism circumvented by voting, even free voting. A government mandated by majority vote becomes factional if it harasses the minority of non-supporters. We should remember that the Nazi faction – its sinister intentions perfectly obvious – was voted into power. In all this, Burke's anti-factionalism is vindicated.

Burke Would Have Seen Communism and Nazism as Allied Phenomena

A man with Burke's acumen would have sided with modern writers like Richard Pipes who claim that Fascist totalitarianism, and still more Nazi totalitarianism, so far from constituting a philosophical opposite to Communism were, at root, Marxist heresies (Pipes 1994).[2] They were not precisely the same as Communism, but even so, very similar. They shared the same savage antinomianism and addiction to bogus science, the same passion for false theories of historical salvation, for whose errors millions of innocent souls have paid an exorbitant price in suffering and death. They were, in their ideational essence, the spawn of the French Revolution. It is true that compared to Hitler or Stalin, Mussolini looks like an amateur totalitarian today, though, ironically, it was Italian theorists who invented the term 'totalitarian' (Pipes 1994: 243).[3]

Under Burkean Eyes: The Crudity of Our Modern Political Discourse

There have been many admirable writings in the free societies, devoted to the totalitarian era. What we have not always grasped, and Burke would have noticed, is that the appreciation of totalitarianism requires that we develop a distinct philosophy and sociology for the understanding of its governance. What would perhaps most have offended Burke about modern politics in the free societies, had he been able to observe us, is that where government is concerned, we live in an intellectually crude culture in which 'politics' is understood as a universal co-term for the machinations of 'power' rather than as a sophisticated and austere process for its management and containment. Politics is a *special form* of government (Crick 1993). Burke might well call it priceless. It emerged in Great Britain in the eighteenth century and was also entrenched in the British North America, where, indeed, it emerged strengthened by the struggle for American independence.

It is a tolerant mode of governance. It insists on the rule of law and admits the existence of sharply differing interests. These may be irreconcilable and thus require permanent, mutual tolerance. Where they can be reconciled, civilized discourse is required. All this is laid out in Crick's famous book. This form of governance is now gradually spreading around the world, alongside the market economy. In Burke's day the mode was at least implicitly opposed by the ideologues of 'rational' revolution in France, with their unlimited claims. Therein is the core reason for Burke's detestation of these ideas. An untried theory of unlimited ambition was being preferred to a provenly workable evolution.

Intellectual crudity is probably inevitable given that the problem of governance concerns all men, and that in a society professing concern for all its members, indeed for the whole human race, we are bound to reach for a universal vocabulary. Even so, this search generates indiscriminate identifications, often a source more of confusion than enlightenment.

As Crick said, in some ways we are less sophisticated in understanding our society than were our eighteenth-century forbears (ibid.). To say of British or American politics on the one hand, and Nigerian or Burmese 'politics' on the other, for example, that the differences are merely versions of the same thing, is to put a burden on the words 'merely' and 'politics' which they cannot legitimately bear. The same consideration holds entirely – it seems – for all the phenomena of totalitarianism, many now happily on the wane. In the totalitarian era, to speak of politics as a universal problem, which happened to be solved in one way by the free societies and in another by the Hitlers and Stalins, was to cut politics off as a concept from the imperatives of decency.

Not everyone will err so crudely, but precisely that crude tendency is the drift caused by the vocabulary. 'Politics' becomes, rather than the name for a *special* kind of governance, one subject to the limits on which Burke always insisted, a co-term for *governance in general.* We engage widely in this error. Let us reinforce the point. It abuses words to call the non-negotiable control and management of totalitarian dinosaurs like China or Cuba or North Korea by their inner party elites, 'politics', as if that management bore close relation to political discourse and interchange in the United States or Great Britain.[4]

The governance of these Marxist oddities, backwaters like Cuba or North Korea, or the astounding new hybrid market economy presided over by a dysfunctional ideological rump of aged rent-seekers,[5] in 'Communist' China, is neither *of* nor *by* nor *for* the populace. This absence of a proper citizenry defined the now – thank God – fading totalitarian episode. It also defined its forerunners, the Jacobin faction, so well described and explained by Burke.

The West's Alleged Triumphalist Pride

It is often asserted that the West, especially the English-speaking West, disdains non-Western cultures, seeking to impose on them its triumphalism, its globalizing capitalism. In America and Britain and throughout all the Western societies, a powerful ideological clique has long been haranguing us on these lines. This was the case put by the French neo-Marxist, the late Pierre Bourdieu. Most of Bourdieu's writing is vitiated by his ferociously dense terminology. His underlying theme, however, is that Western Economics is only a passing construct of Western society (Bourdieu 1998). A version of the same case is advanced by John Gray. He argues that liberal market Economics is only an aspect of the Enlightenment Project, as was Marxism. It now serves as an ideological adjunct to an *offensive* American triumphalism (Gray 1998).

The neo-Cons in the United States *have* exemplified a triumphalist praise of the market economy and universal franchise, as if they constituted a universal terminus for human history. American governments do not proclaim this, however. Western officialdom has not insulted non-Western societies thus. Gray's claim is, in this respect, as false as Bourdieu's. Modern Western governments *rarely* despise non-Western societies blatantly. More often they are much too kind to them. Consider the lengths to which Western countries will go to propitiate Muslim countries and Muslim people. Burke would have despised such propitiation. In his day he was against the French Revolution. In the twentieth century he would have opposed totalitarianism. Today he would be against Islamism. But Burke also opposes Western societies which *underestimate* their worth. We have forgotten Burke's forthright honesty. He pulled no punches in his courteous writing to the young French gentleman to whom his *Reflections* was directed.

> You began ill, because you began by despising everything that belonged to you. (Burke 1790)

The point is Burke's honesty. Neither past sins nor ancient virtue must be denied. Such honesty exemplifies the truth that the West is the only culture ever to have cast a severe, openended critical eye on its past. The first and only civilization to have abolished slavery is also the only one to have pondered its burden of guilt or its unique achievement in this regard. All his life Burke opposed slavery. We are the legatees of such clear-sightedness. Slavery was vile, and the British eventually repudiated it. Sadly, in the case of some very important countries today, we do not today speak to their controlling groups with the frankness we owe them, either about past or present sins. We should be straight with them, for good or for bad.

The West and Its Economics

In any case, *pace* John Gray, the superiority of Western economics is not so much an ideology as a fact. The English-speaking West alone has recognized Economics as no more than the logic of scarcity, best conducted in free markets. This is the Economics of Adam Smith, to which his friend Burke subscribed. The state, Smith believed, should keep out. No modern state does; the question is relative. Those societies which have most heeded Smith's view – most English-speaking ones now have in varying degree and some non-English speaking ones too – while like all societies they have severe periodic difficulties, tend to surmount them. This is discernible even within our present, frightening economic doldrums. The economic woes of Japan, France and Germany long pre-date these. It will be interesting to see whether the difficulties apparent at present will be better surmounted by India, with its entrepreneurial free enterprise, or China with its state-managed capitalism.

India, a Triumph of East and West

We rightly praise India. India is the non-European society which today most deserves compliments for its constitutionality. Burke had never been there but regarded Indian civilization highly. India is by a long way the most populous law-state the world has ever seen. It is a beacon of the reviving power of the Orient. It is entirely appropriate that on 4th June 2008, one of Burke's most notable enthusiasts today, Paul Johnson (2008*a*), in the course of the IEA annual Hayek Memorial lecture, proposed that India will overtake China economically and politically because she is a free society.

Civilization and Its Moral
Confrontation with the Past

Would not Burke insist, however, that it is not enough to provide a model for economic emulation, however useful that may be? The fundamental Burkean imperative is surely enlightened governance. Are the advanced cultures not remiss in failing to criticize sufficiently the dangerous refusal of societies like China, Russia and Japan to confront their appalling recent pasts? China has, rather more than Russia, followed the example of Japan in acceding to the idea of private business. None of these very important countries seems truly willing, however, to look at their vast, recent criminality. There must needs be a purgation, a severe one, if they are to pass on, as Burke says is a prime duty of the living, decent standards to their posterity. In respect of this crucial issue, the West has been mealy-mouthed in its dealings, rather than frank and courageous, let alone bombastic and triumphalist, as Gray alleges.

China sells us manufactures and Russia oil and gas. This is an advance on Communism. But if Western statesmen are resolute, Burke's ghost will confront the continuing shortcomings of these societies. They will not belong fully to civilization until their leaderships submit their modern history of murder and nihilism to proper scrutiny (O'Keeffe 2007: 32–9). Nor do the Japanese seem open to looking at the grisly record of their former empire. Peoples wishing to enter the lighted circle of civilization must put the moral searchlights on. Polite critical observation is not intolerable 'neo-Con' intervention.

The Advanced Free Societies Have Inherited Some
of Their Factionalism from the Totalitarian Episode

The free societies have to deal domestically, not with totalitarianism proper but with the dangerous legacy its thinking has left in our midst. Most insidious is the factionalism which now infects so many areas of our public life. Factionalism is inherent in human affairs. It did not start with totalitarianism. Nor does it all come from Marxism and its allied perspectives, although these were history's most extreme version of the malady. In the last century, a dangerous admiration for Communism was widespread in the free societies. This eventuality would have appalled Burke.

Totalitarian Perspectives as the Abolition of History

Historical discontinuities can be good or bad. The Industrial Revolution was overwhelmingly benign. It broke with (progressively discontinued) the poverty of the past; but unlike the Reformation did not deliberately seek to cut off the population from their traditions and history, or at least never advisedly. Communism and Nazism were horrible discontinuities which deliberately cut off the present from the past. This kind of outcome is what Burke suspected and alleged of eighteenth-century France. Roger Scruton explains Burke as seeing 'social order as a partnership, in which the dead and the unborn are included along with the living' (Scruton 1994: 417). This entails a living sense of history.

Today our history is again under attack. We in the West may be even more vulnerable than the Post-Communist populations. *We do not know how much totalitarian ideas have affected us.* In those parts of our economic system which are publicly financed, a writ-small but many faceted version of the abolition of history is now widely institutionalized. Our religion, our marriages, our law, our intellectual self-understanding – all these are now under threat. As should be clear by now, the aim of a Burkean philosophy of government is that the good of the past shall live on in the present and be handed on by its present beneficiaries to their children.

The very worst Western attempt at the abolition of history is the one mounted by the European Union faction in its aim to demolish the nations of Europe in favour of a super-state. Burke would have despised the British luminaries who have supported this gross attack on our history and political culture, which they have greatly compounded by a now out of control mass immigration.

Factions and Public Finance

Our descendants, if they live in free societies, will need the guidance of many wise and virtuous persons, past and present, to secure and perpetuate that admirable condition. They will look to the political records of patriotic giants like Churchill, Truman, De Gaulle, Reagan and Thatcher. In the matter of writers who defended freedom, Burke will perhaps be thought by some to deserve pride of place.

Burke would have concurred with opponents of the disastrous ease with which factions in America and Britain can get access to public funds. He would surely be astounded at the vast torrents of public money available for factional causes. Under the influence of what we earlier called 'rightsology' the intellectuals of the public sector have stirred up hatred between the sexes, between the races and between cultures and religions. The 'rights' about which they prattle are all in the eighteenth-century French tradition, based on purely abstract and loose speculation, with no thought given to the consequences of over-concentrating on such questions, no care for the impact of these ideas if they are institutionalized. They all result in factional lobbies. Our descendants, if they enjoy free commentary, will be amazed at our governments' casual prodigality with other people's earnings. Government by the lobby system often, indeed usually, means government assailed by groups armed financially with the proceeds of public taxation and constantly demanding more. Even in free societies our governments treat our money as though it were theirs.

Factions can, demonstrably, burrow their way into wide public concerns: education, health, race-relations, relations between the sexes, relations between the cultures, broadcasting and many, many more. As Paul Johnson has pointed out in *The Spectator* (London), the Greens are the most powerful lobby in the world today. They are active at ground level, having put in a huge appearance in our primary schools. Their fantasy of global warming, says Johnson, is a religious surrogate (Johnson 2008*b*: 24). If they get their way, they will condemn to poverty millions of people round the world whom the spontaneous forces of the market would lift from that condition if they were allowed to operate freely. Similarly, the Rousseau fantasy of 'progressive education' imposed on schools and teacher preparation by ruthless romantics likewise condemns millions of children in countries like the United States, Great Britain and Australia, to illiteracy, innumeracy and moral vacuity. It is scarcely necessary to ask what Burke would have thought of this.

Factions and the Faltering of Religion

For Burke the central cause of faction and sectarian obsessions was the decay in religion. We adverted to this in Chapter 3. The *Second Letter on a Regicide Peace* (1796*b*) puts faction at the heart of the revolutionary prospectus. Note in the extract below, to which reference was also made in Chapter 3, that the word 'sect' is a synonym for faction:

> . . . the Jacobins . . . saw the thing right from the very beginning. Whatever were the first motives to the war among politicians, they saw that it is in its spirit, and for its objects, a *civil war;* and as such they pursued it. It is a war between the partisans of the ancient, civil, moral, and political order of Europe against a *sect* (my italics) of fanatical and ambitious atheists which means to change them all. It is not France extending a foreign empire over other nations: it is a *sect* aiming at universal empire, and beginning with the conquest of France. (Burke 1796*b*: 3)

Western affluence, spearheaded by American military might, science and technology, has reduced Communist power to dust. But given the passion some people have for domination over others and even for their own reduction to servitude, the impulses which produced the Communist afflatus may be expected to exert themselves indefinitely. It is even possible that the West has won the battles of the Cold War, but lost the war itself.

The West Is Infected Ideologically, Crucially in Its Education Systems

Burke's uncanny, perhaps one should say 'unique', prescience, allowed him to foresee the totalitarian experience in shadowy but already fearful outline. What we have not raised thus far, however, is the astonishing influence in our free societies, often unrecognized, of precisely the kind of ideological thinking and organization which led to the totalitarian regimes.

The religious tradition has in good measure held its own in the United States. The tragic decline during the twentieth century and on into the twenty-first, in Great Britain, Australia, and today even in Burke's native Ireland, would greatly have alarmed him. We have cleared out the larger nests of Communism. It no longer degrades whole nations. But its ideological spirit – a relentless antinomianism – still commands vast resources as its medium, in its new redoubts in the public sectors of the free societies.

In fact, the educational sub-systems of America and Britain have an internal power structure and an economic modus operandi very like that of a Communist state. How did this come to pass, in the very societies which defeated Nazism and Communism? It is a consequence of the control of our educational arrangements, our cultural transmission, by inefficient but sinister factions. Proper things, like the teaching of literacy and numeracy are done inadequately for decades on end.

Improper things, like worrying children about their race or sex, continue their disastrous course for years. Fortunately our educational arrangements in America and Britain are constrained by the surrounding legitimacy of the rule of law and the workings of free enterprise. They are preserved therefore from the full horrors which education in totalitarian societies entailed. Even so they are very bad, stuck as they are in a stasis of catchword slogans and policy malfunctions and dysfunctions, in which words proper are drained of all real substance and activities come to seem very like a perpetual mimicry of the French Revolution and its offspring, minus the murder.

The words of the best-known educational trade unionist in America, the late Albert Shanker, are very revealing here. Shanker was till late in the day virtually a Marxist. He says, quite baldly, that the American school-system:

> . . . operates like a planned economy . . . it's no surprise our school system doesn't improve . . . it resembles the Communist economy. (Shanker 1986)

Our educational malaise flows from the educational disenfranchisement of a very large part of the population. The problem, as a very sizeable literature shows, is that the mass education systems of modern free societies are run largely for the convenience of their leaderships and the promulgation of their ideological fantasies. There are insufficient opportunities for exit by dissatisfied customers. Lots of people cannot afford to pay for private schooling for their children. Many cannot afford to buy houses where the schools are good. Low standards can and do therefore persist for decades on end.

Burke's thinking is thus today most significant for the analysis of education. In our educational arrangements we see the most lethal of the 'totalitarian residua' which disfigure free societies like the United States and Great Britain, Australia and many more. The near monopoly of public finance in educational and other public services, together with a mix of egalitarian and pseudo-scientific ideologies, constitutes their socialism. In the commercial economy, citizens have a sound grip on what is produced, through their direct purchases. Shanker is quite right, therefore, though we might replace his 'Communist' with the less alarming epithet 'socialist'.

It is notable how much modern so-called scholarship has attacked the very basis of our society. Along with the Marxism which so foolishly scorned our private enterprise economy, have gone attacks on fundamental institutions like the family. It is the bonds of family and friendship which hold society together at the local level and which transmute over time and under lawful government into a larger patriotism. As Burke says:

. . . to love the little platoon we belong to is the first principle (the germ as it were) of public affections. (Burke 1790)

In America the word 'liberal' disguises the *socialist facts.* Mostly, of course, the educational leadership of American and British schooling want to control us, in particular to cut us off from our histories. This is not the developed malice of totalitarianism proper, but it is a pathology on the same road. We now return to the theme of the contemporary attempt at the abolition of history, hoping to find Burke's inspiration here also.

Nineteen Eighty-Four and All That: Education and the Abolition of History

That our posterity will suffer if we neglect our ancestors is a constant Burkean theme. It is not clear who first proposed that totalitarian governance is centrally predicated on the abolition of history, but an obvious starting point is Orwell's *Nineteen Eighty-Four.* Fortunately, the year in question has come and gone, and we, in the advanced societies, are still here, still relatively affluent, relatively free. This by no means deprives Orwell's brilliantly executed fable of its explanatory force. One weakness of his text is that it argues only for the terrifying *outcomes* of the manipulation of mind by an utterly unaccountable elite. It does not argue how this purpose might be achieved; it does not look at its main agency: mass education.

Mass Education and the Fantasy of Children's Happiness

Our educational arrangements would have greatly offended Burke. We have the wealth and technical means to create high standards of education. Just as Burke would have spotted the moral collapse in our politics, so too would he have homed in on the intimately related collapse in education. Huge numbers of the people who have passed through American and British schools in the last three decades can neither read nor write nor calculate properly. Many also have little in the way of a moral compass. One cannot look at these facts without concluding that the elite in charge of education is dishonest and corrupt, as well as obstinate in its refusal of the evidence. The market economy could not work if its leading lights were comparably remiss. Moreover, while market failure, even when it is disastrous in scale, is episodic, public sector failures like education are virtually continuous.

Burke would also have certainly recognized the influence of his bête noire, Rousseau, in these shortcomings. Were Burke's ghost to wander disconsolately down the corridors of modern academia, he would unerringly pick out Rousseau as the worst of eighteenth-century France's *terribles simplificateurs*. In the twentieth century Dewey was a comparable nuisance in his influence on the American schoolroom. The central error bequeathed us from these sources is the attempt to marry education to a search for child happiness.

Only incidentally, for Burke, could education be about children's development, let alone their happiness. The very idea is an ahistorical heresy, which Burke would roundly reprove. For Christians the telos of human history is not happiness but moral order. Education should have two purposes: the reproduction of virtue and the transmission and expansion of knowledge. These do still operate, of course, but very much sub-optimally, and they are certainly not the main preoccupation of the system. Nor, incidentally, is there any evidence that the pursuit of children's happiness via such wrong theories makes them happy. Nor would Burke have been fooled by the dishonest and dysfunctional contemporary expansion in *higher* education in America and Great Britain (Johnson 1984: 641–5).[6]

Burke and the Miasma in Tertiary Education

Sociology can be illuminating. Of what value, however, are the antinomian versions of it taught so widely today? Much of the content of the higher education curriculum is useless. Obsessive subjects like 'media studies' have been widely pursued. This has in turn affected even the schooling of little children when teachers see fit to harass them with questions such as what colour they are and to which sex – or to use the false synonym 'gender' – they belong. The rationale for expansion of the education system overall is in the most naïve 'more education equals economic growth' vein.

Prudent Commonplaces and Suspicious Fantasies

Burke never loses sight of the civilized commonplaces. He would otherwise be a strange kind of political animal, as men like Rousseau and Marx were, indeed, strange, in their day. It is also notable that Burke does not defer to Plato in the way he does to Aristotle.[7] Perhaps he thought of Plato in the same way he thought of Rousseau – as a bully out to promote an artificial society. The champions of modern intellectual relativism, the harbingers of chaos, people like Foucault and Derrida, were also strange in *our* era. The influence of these two men in the universities of the free world has been extraordinary in the last thirty years. Foucault's essential position was a nihilist rejection of all hierarchy (Foucault 1977). For much of his life he attacked the very centre of the tradition of Christian humanism, namely the idea of the human subject. For him the individual was a figment from an oppressive text. Derrida's principal claim – made in obscurantist jargon – is that all language is corrupt, soaked in the interests of sexual and racial oppression (Derrida 1992).

These thinkers all preferred the odd convention of interpreting everything as if it were something else. This reflects the suspicion of the world which Rousseau and Marx fostered. This lingers on today, though happily the wider Communist program is now abandoned. Such a convention – routine suspicion – is strange, because all intellectual creation, and perhaps above all creativity in matters pertaining to human governance, demands a scrupulous attention to the human world and its realities. Involving as it does, an interchange between the will and intellect of individuals and the world in which the owners of these capacities find themselves, intellectual activity needs realism, sense and caution, in a word, prudence, as well as inspiration. These men whom I have named – Voltaire, Rousseau, Marx, Foucault and Derrida – did not pursue that prudence. In the case of all of them, caution is missing. Their work is dominated by their own perverse and ungovernable wills. They are all antinomians, treasuring, publicly, the unbearable sweetness of their sensibility. All seek to tear down the world and start anew. They pursue their own furious demons, whatever the consequences.

The German Communist playwright, Berthold Brecht, spoke tellingly for this perversity, when it was still unambiguously mortgaged to Communism: 'sink into the mud, and embrace the butcher; but change the world; it needs it' (Brecht 1931). Those who wish fundamentally to preserve are scrupulous in the attention they pay to things external to their imaginations.

Burke never forgets our human realities. It is the observation of this by his readers which has led to his being falsely labelled a utilitarian. Utilitarianism was never so imaginative nor so salient. Burke possessed in abundance the gift of salience, the ability to pick out the *key points* of a situation or set of events. And what he picked out in relation to the goings-on in France is immediately familiar to the student of modern totalitarianism. More important, and less well-known, I have tried to show, is the relevance of his findings to the free societies.

Burke and the Rejection of Fatalism

Nor has the attack on Christianity been a purely spiritual matter. As we have argued earlier, Christianity, with its doctrine of the individual soul, has been crucial in the emergence of individualism, and in turn of personal responsibility as a theme in moral discourse. These notions supply the background to the non-fatalistic attitude to history characterizing the West. Non-fatalism is crucial to the Burkean outlook, and today crucial to the West's claim to civilized status. Fatalism typifies Islam, just as it also typifies the socialistic mindset of those who control the welfare state in the free societies. Much in the manner of the Communist state, our education clings to provenly false methods long after their sell-by date. 'Special Needs', for example, is largely special pleading for children not having been taught to read. Their illiteracy follows from a wrong method of teaching reading (Buckard 2007).

Relativism against History and Patriotism

The very worst feature of modern education in the free societies is the growth and pervasiveness of intellectual relativism. This represents entrenched commitment to intellectual error. It could not survive if the populations were better educated, particularly if they knew more history. It has been shown time and again that the populations of the advanced societies are shockingly ignorant of the past. What is missing is any precise knowledge of the background to this ignorance.

We know that anti-imperialism is understandably but also rather naively institutionalized in the United States. This is a legacy of the War of Independence. Why it should have been so strong in the British case for most of the last century is less clear. We do know that many people in education in both countries believe that their histories are morally repugnant. A similar view informs the outlook of many Australian intellectuals too. Perhaps this is all a function of the Protestant guilt-culture. Perhaps too even the excesses of this culture are preferable to the cult of shame which prevents some notable cultures from properly examining their pasts. How though is our self-denigration achieved?

My colleague at the former Polytechnic of North London, Donald Hill, did once show that the working-party set up in London to discuss the development of 'Urban Studies' in the first half of the 1980s, took pains to make sure the program was Marxianized (Hill 1985). What is happening now that Marxism has been dumped, effectively, is a matter for investigation.

Burke on Relativism

A well-educated guess would have Burke identifying intellectual relativism as the central cognitive and moral pathology of the advanced free societies, a cult which has undermined the traditional distinction – found in all the great civilizations – between civilization and barbarism. At its starkest, the relativist cult holds that no hierarchies, whether governmental, social, intellectual, aesthetic or religious, have any intrinsic legitimacy, positions high and low in such hierarchies all being decided and upheld, entirely and only, by the imperatives of mere power. If American and British politics is anything to go by, the whole thesis is nonsense. Much of the political leadership of these two countries in the last hundred years has come from *humble* beginnings.

Burke would surely have shared Allan Bloom's dismay that at a great institution of learning like the University of Chicago, by the late 1980s, the standard view among the students was that nothing can be regarded as better than anything else, in any aspect of human endeavour (Bloom 1988). This view helps to endorse the crippling philistinism of mass culture. Nor has much been said about the moronizing dialectic between mass entertainment and our socialist education systems, with their low standards, whose very worst feature is the intellectual relativism which reigns in them. What we have, functionally, however few people have noticed, is a kind of conspiracy between educational socialism and the worst kind of business people (O'Keeffe 1998).

It would have been good to hear Burke on relativism. Relativism has been more or less orthodoxy in much modern governmental practice in the advanced English-speaking societies. For decades, before its present collapse in Britain, for example, multiculturalism reigned supreme in educational administration. 'Radical' scholars in America have enthused over the most degenerate popular music. A certain Melanie Morton used to enthuse, says Robert Hughes, over Madonna, to the effect that her melodies 'prevent ideological closure' and that 'she rejects core bourgeois epistemes' (Hughes 1993: 69). In teacher education there may have been opponents of the relativist orthodoxy – I myself was a vociferous one (O'Keeffe 1990) – but they mostly kept their heads below the parapet. To question multiculturalism and the related obsessions of anti-racism, feminism, anti-imperialism and so on, was to court promotional and career disaster.

Relativism as used today – to mean that there are no genuine hierarchies – is actually misconceived. In the traditional sense the notion of the relative is an entirely orthodox and indispensable one, in the ways in which it is applied to ethics or art or military prowess or any other human activity. Some individuals, some acts, some national achievements, some sciences, are superior to others. Let us consider, among an infinity of examples, the idea that, when the Europeans found them, the Aboriginals of New Zealand were at a higher state of culture than those of Australia.

Burke would have appreciated this claim. Indeed, he made such comparisons effortlessly. Burke would have had no truck with such nonsense as pretending there is no such thing as civilization or barbarism. In his 'An Address to the British Colonists in North America', he assures the Colonists that the best Englishmen would certainly not consider loosing on them 'fierce tribes of savages and cannibals' (Burke 1972*a*: 166). Does the term 'savages' not fit today the Taliban and Al' Qaeda?

Similarly, Burke knew that there are bad empires and good ones. Indeed, to defend his thesis that the British Empire was benign, Burke would have needed to compare it, and perhaps did compare it, to empires which were worse or even appallingly so.

Burke on Nations, Empires and Modernity

Robin Harris notes that General de Gaulle regarded nations as the only reality of modern politics (Harris 2008). It is scarcely better than a commonplace to observe that Burke would have agreed, and that he regarded the British, and especially the English, as the greatest of all nations. An admiration for pre-Revolutionary France is also apparent. Burke sees empires as a significant reality too. In fact Burke was a passionate believer in empires *and* nations, provided they were good empires and good nations. He would have excoriated the reflex hostility that nation and empire have aroused among modern bien-pensant intellectuals in Britain during the last 150 years. He would also disdain the adversarial, anti-patriotic attitude of many Americans and Australians.

Burke's support of empire as a political form stemmed mainly from his conviction that the British Empire was a benign force in the world. There are outstanding modern historians who would agree, as we saw in earlier chapters.

Burke is not, however, in the least ingenuous. He knows some nations and some empires are evil. Can we doubt that Burke would have welcomed the defeat of Carthage by Rome, for example? 'Cartago delenda est' – Carthage must be destroyed – is an imperative of the kind often repeated in history. Burke would also undoubtedly have seen the hand of divine providence behind the successive failures of the East to overwhelm Europe. The Persian, the Carthaginian, the Hunnic, the Arab/Islamic, the Mongol/Turkic menaces – all failed ultimately, just as the Islamist movements will fail, according to Michael Burleigh's fine book (Burleigh 2008*a*: xi). I speak in terms of repetition, here, of course, not of continuity of purpose. There is no place called the 'East' consistently seeking over the centuries to overwhelm another place called the 'West'.

In the matter of empires Burke would have noticed some of the important imperial features of the modern world and its recent past:

1. There are good empires and bad ones.
2. There are examples of sound polities, benign societies, which do not recognize their imperial character. The United States is one such. The American belief that the country is not imperial is probably politic. The blanket American rejection of all other imperialism, however, and the American pressure on Europe to disengage from its possessions in Africa and elsewhere after the Second World War, was an error for which millions of people have paid a terrible price. Burke would have said that the British, French and Portuguese should have stayed much longer in Africa.

Would not Burke also, however, have accepted the following?

3. There are evil empires which repudiate the idea that they are imperial dispensations. The Soviet Union was such.
4. There are evil empires which admit as much. The shorter-lived Nazi system, the Third Reich, was an avowedly evil empire.
5. Empires often function to diffuse and endorse many welcome aspects of the free society and economy, internationally, with specific intention to resist and reverse the encroachment of barbarous systems of governance. Recourse is sometime made to military resistance.

In recent centuries this claim applies dramatically to Britain and even more to the United States. Some important thinkers have offended in the free societies by wrongly construing empire as a political form, damning the good with bad. Burke's friend, Adam Smith was one. Frédéric Bastiat was a notable offender too. Bastiat has a magnificent understanding of the moral dynamics of a free society, and its attendant free market, but his hostility to empire as a political form seems blind to the fact that in the absence of European empires these free market ideas could not possibly have gained a strong institutional purchase (Bastiat 1995).

Islamism and the Absence of a Free Citizenry

In our discussion of the totalitarian phenomenon, we kept one crucial topic separate, because it is a potential totalitarian variant, not yet instantiated in the world. Interestingly it would if it materialized, prove to be an Imperial totalitarianism, rather than a national one. The same absence of a free citizenry which we earlier noted as characterizing socialist totalitarianism, now holds for those states or movements – 'virtual states in fact' – under the heretical version of Islam which now aspires to rule the world. Islamism conforms utterly to the proposition that totalitarianism has no proper politics in the Crickian sense that we discussed earlier. Modern politics proper has emancipated women and has insisted that parents do not own children, since no one can properly own someone else. It is this moral understanding which Islamism seeks to reverse, just as secular modern totalitarianism sought to establish its assumption that individuals are, effectively, the property of the state. Fortunately, most Muslims are not hateful. We have to conclude, however, that if Al Qaeda did succeed in establishing a new Caliphate, this would be a totalitarian replacement for Communism. Philip Bobbitt, fortunately, finds this unlikely (Bobbitt and Gove 2008: 31).

Burke and Burleigh: The Need for Clarity of Vision and Courage

Burke would surely have said that those Muslim clerics, living in the advanced societies, who preach scorn for our free society and encourage its subversion and overthrow, should be subject to severe treatment by the law. It is not clear, however, that the establishments in the free societies today have the stomach for such confrontation. Indeed the cowardice of these establishments shames us all. Burke would favour the robust, clear-sighted policy advocated by Michael Burleigh in *Standpoint* (Burleigh 2008*b*: 34–7). Our intelligence should sort out the majority Muslim wheat from the minority chaff, worldwide. British policy should cut off the subversive financial flows from Saudi, and elsewhere, and imitate the more robust resistance France is now showing to Islamism.

A Final Note: Burke and Harvey Mansfield and Even Higher Authority

It seems unlikely that a wise world will ever safely be able to dispense with wisdom and insight of the Burke sort. A fine echo of Burke is found in Harvey Mansfield's well-known view that modern Western man's central error is the hubristic belief that there is nothing greater than us. We do not know if nemesis will ever overtake us, though intellectual pessimists never seem to find difficulty in locating candidates to deliver the ultimate *coup de grace* to an erring humanity. Climate, resources and demographics have been the favourite fads for the last two centuries. It is hard to imagine that Burke would have taken their overblown status seriously, except as evidence of intellectual pathology. They rise and fall with such risible speed. Burke possessed an intelligence such as to make most humans seem like very ordinary clay. He himself would have said that the truth about the future – nemesis or otherwise – is known only to an infinitely greater intelligence than his own.

Notes

Chapter 1

[1] The Nagle family today believes that the Richard who converted to Anglicanism was the father of Edmund. O'Brien believes they are right.

[2] Friel, Brian in his play *Translations*.

[3] See also Burke, E. (1982).

[4] Anarchism is fundamentally the doctrine that all government is oppressive.

[5] Friel, Brian in his play *Translations*.

[6] The details of Burke's argument are actually controversial as we shall see in a later chapter.

[7] O'Brien writes, with a kind of poetic licence, some pages on the ills of the system of tenure in nineteenth-century Ireland, in his book on Burke's Irish writings. Burke's eighteenth-century writings, however, have little to say on the tenure problem. See O'Brien in Burke, E. *Irish Affairs* Introduction, pp. viii–xx.

[8] 'Let no man dare, when I am dead, charge me with dishonour'. See, *www.hoganstand.com/general/identity/extras/patriots/stories/robertemmet*.

[9] A speech before the House of Commons during the debate on the address of thanks, 13 November 1770.

[10] Such optimism remains a central flaw in liberalism.

Chapter 2

[*] The title 'Genial Olympian' is intended to draw the reader's attention to the remarkable warmth which suffuses Burke's writings, adding a winning and persuasive charm to whatever degree of explanatory power he achieves. As the first chapter made clear he is

regarded as an intellectual giant in some circles and as an establishment hack in others. This author is officially constrained to stay well
clear of idolatry in his intellectual account. No such constraint holds,
however, on the issue of his human attractiveness.

1 Let me remind the reader that the Stuarts were the first dynasty to
   rule in Scotland as well as England and Wales.

2 The main purpose of Burke's 1784 speech A Representation to his
   Majesty was to control expenditure, and especially to limit the growth
   of the Civil List.

3 In the next half decade Liberty Fund of Indianapolis will be publishing all Bastiat's work in six volumes, a project this author has been
   involved in.

4 See chapter titled 'A Letter to Richard Burke'.

5 Burke makes a number of references to Dr Richard Price, a noncon-
   formist Minister.

6 Canavan, F. (1960) *The Political Reason of Edmund Burke*, Durham, NC:
   Duke University Press, p. 45.

7 A Notebook of Edmund Burke, Cambridge, 1957 in Canavan
   (1960).

8 Johnson had actually said, 'If Pope be not a poet, where is poetry to
   be found?'

9 It was surely in the spirit of such thinking that one of Burke's most
   eminent modern admirers, Paul Johnson, proposed in his Institute
   of Economic Affairs, Hayek Memorial Lecture ['Freeholds and Property: The Importance of Private Property in Promoting and Securing
   Liberty], on 4 June 2008, that India would eventually overhaul China
   in economic development and political power. Johnson is proposing
   that freedom and right conduct will prove invincible.

10 The book's full title, however, is: *Reflections on the Revolution in France*.
   The term 'French Revolution' is not used by Burke.

11 The name of the Radical clergyman, Dr Richard Price, whom Burke
   regarded as an incendiary subversive, appears repeatedly in the text
   and the man is actually discussed on page six.

12 By 'secular' piety I mean reverence and affection for one's history,
   nation, language and generally tried and trusted traditions.

13 The word 'metaphysics' has a huge range of meanings. It may mean
   the contemplation of things which are higher and more primal than
   man in the scheme of existence. It may mean the guiding idea of a
   branch of knowledge, for example 'natural selection' in Darwinian
   biology, or 'utility maximization' in economics. Its everyday sense,
   still in use, is the one Burke employs. For Burke it means ideas and
   speculations which are out of touch with practical realities.

¹⁴ Reflections in *Works V*, 303n.
¹⁵ 'Thou, Nature art my Goddess'. *King Lear* Act I scene 2.
¹⁶ Montesquieu had denied Hobbes's state of nature.
¹⁷ *Hamlet* Act V scene 2.
¹⁸ Condorcet's belief in a scientific political administration is one example.
¹⁹ Burke was a very enlightened man in the dictionary sense of the word. He did not trust the new Continental rationalism, however. The English and Scottish Enlightenment was much more deeply touched by Christian thinking than the continental variety. Voltaire was brilliant, but unlike Burke he was not perceptive in a deep way. Burke understood that the French Enlightenment aimed at the overthrow of religion, which in turn portended the overthrow of the whole existing constitutional order.
²⁰ For a brilliant, advanced, though not very well indexed treatment of the substance of my last paragraph, see Canavan (1960).

Chapter 3

¹ For a brilliant discussion of (mainly) German revolutionary thinking in this period, see Kolakowski, L. (1978).
² Utilitarianism: the doctrine that human actions, morals and institutions, are most appropriately and meaningfully judged by how useful they are and to how many people.
³ McCue is referring to Schama (1990) which was a huge, well-received book.
⁴ The Prelude has a long section on the genius of Burke.
⁵ See the back cover of O'Brien (1997)
⁶ Part One especially, but see also Parts Two and Three.
⁷ In his commentary on Burke. See Burke, E. (1975) *On Government, Politics and Society*, edited and with an introduction by Hill, B.W. Harvester in conjunction with Fontana, op.cit p. 276.
⁸ Dryden's exact words are: "Great wits are sure to madness near allied, And thin partitions do their bounds divide". *Absalom and Achitophel*, 1681, is widely thought of as the greatest political poem in English.
⁹ There is little left of the reason or the science either, following the totalitarian horrors. We are left with a large intellectually bereft group of scholars, who will not read Burke, or others readers of his stripe, for reasons no longer supporting any viable political orientation.

[10] *Le Petit Robert* 1967, p. 290. This is the shorter version of the standard dictionary of the French language.

[11] In this sense 'bourgeois' dates from 1674, see *Shorter English Oxford Dictionary* (1972) p. 209.

[12] From Book X

[13] From Book XII.

[14] This outlook is merely central doctrine in Christian outlooks.

[15] I owe it to my readers to point out that Professor David Conway, who much admires Burke, has observed that Price enjoys quite a high reputation intellectually in the history of thought, that he was not nearly as subversive as Burke suggests and that Adam Smith, who also disliked him, actually made use of some of his work. Of course Price's grotesque chortling over the humiliation of Louis XVI remains unpardonable, but he is not in general terms the dangerous and also second-rate monster Burke portrays. See Conway, D. (2004) pp. 153–5.

[16] In both cases what is implied are low moral standards and lack of scruple or proper conscience.

[17] Plato proposes an austere, philistine republic, run by 'Guardians', people of pure character who will organize the lives of unintelligent folk on wholesome lines. They are empowered to lie to these lesser souls on prudential grounds. Burke shares nothing with Plato.

[18] Arthur Koestler, *Darkness at Noon*; George Orwell, *Nineteen Eighty-Four*; Karl Popper, *The Open Society and Its Enemies*; Friedrich von Hayek, *The Road to Serfdom*; Leszek Kolakowski, *Main Currents of Marxism.*

[19] In private conversation with the author, in the 1980s and1990s, at venues such as academic conferences.

[20] Churchill, W. (1927) From 'Consistency in Politics'. Nash's *Pall Mall Magazine* July 1927. See Churchill Archive at Churchill College Cambridge, CHAR8/202 Permissions to Curtis Brown, Solicitors.

Chapter 4

[1] Burke says that to consolidate what today we call their 'ideology', 'They contrived to possess themselves, with great method and perseverance, of all the avenues to literary fame'.

[2] See chapter 5.

[3] There is something anachronistic about asking a long-dead writer's opinion on events after his death, and on themes whose vocabulary

would have been alien to him. Even so, Burke seems uncannily on the case with these dreadful revisitations from antique slavery. The term 'totalitarian' was coined by Giovanni Amendola, pejoratively, though soon adopted by Mussolini and Gentile, for favourable usage.

4 It is true that in earlier chapters I have not observed my own distinctions. I have indeed treated 'politics' as referring to universal problems of governance. All who write in this intellectual area will be stuck with this difficulty until a new vocabulary able to handle these distinctions emerges.

5 'Dysfunctional' means both 'inadequate' and 'improper'. 'Rent-seekers' is a term from the branch of economic sociology called 'Public Choice'. It refers to employees in the public sector who pursue their own gains instead of the tasks they are employed for, redirecting to their own use the funds officially intended for official purposes. In most Communist societies the Communist party raided the Communist economy. The present Chinese leadership raid the new and much richer market economy.

6 See also, O'Keeffe, D. (1999).

7 Readers might be interested that in preparing this text I found no references by Burke to Plato.

Bibliography

Ashton, T. S. (1964) *The Industrial Revolution, 1760–1830*, London: Oxford University Press.

Barkan, E. (1972) 'Introduction and acknowledgements to Burke, E', *On the American Revolution*, Gloucester, MA: Peter Smith.

Barker, Sir E. (1951) 'Burke on the French Revolution' in *Essays on Government*, Oxford University Press.

Bastiat, F. (1995) 'What is seen and what is not seen' in *Selected Essays in Political Economy*. Irvington on Hudson, NY: The Foundation for Economic Education.

Bastiat, F. (forthcoming) *Thoughts on Sharecropping*, vol. 4, of *The Collected Works of Bastiat*, Indianapolis: Liberty Fund.

Bauer, Lord (1997) *Class on the Brain: The Cost of a British Obsession*, London: Centre for Policy Studies, pp. 1–25.

Berlin, I. (1980) 'L.B. Namier' in *Personal Impressions*, London: Hogarth, pp. 64–5.

Bloom, A. (1988) *The Closing of the American Mind*, New York: Simon & Schuster.

Bobbitt, P. and Gove, M. (2008) 'Rethinking the War on Terror' *Standpoint*, September.

Bourdieu, P. (1998) *Acts of Resistance: Against the Tyranny of the Market*, trans. Richard Nice, New York: New Press.

Brecht, B. (1931) *Die Massnahme (The Measures taken* and other Lehrstucke), London: Eyre Methuen.

Bredvold, L. I. and Ross, R. G. (eds) (1970) 'Prudence as a political virtue' in *The Philosophy of Edmund Burke: A Selection from his Speeches and Writings*. (2nd edn) Ann Arbor: University of Michigan Press.

Buckle, H. T. (1904) *The History of Civilisation in England*. Ed. by John M. Robertson. New York: Dutton.

Burkard, T. (2007) *Inside the Secret Garden: The Progressive Decay of Liberal Education*, Buckingham: University of Buckingham Press.

Burke, E. (1759) *The Annual Register*, London. Vols 2 (1759), 4 (1761), 5 (1762), 14 (1771), 16 (1763).

—(1769) 'Observations on the State of the Nation', in *Works*, vol. 2.

—(1770) *Thoughts on the Causes of the Present Discontents*, Ed. by Henry Morley, The Project Gutenberg eBook.

—(1775) 'Speech on Conciliation with the Colonies' in *Works*, vol. 3, 49–50.

—(1784) 'A Representation to his Majesty' in E. Burke (1975), *On Government, Politics and Society*. Ed. by B. W. Hill. London: Harvester in conjunction with Fontana.

—(1790) *Reflections on the Revolution in France*, The Library of Economics and Freedom, Indianapolis, Liberty Fund.

—(1791) 'Appeal from the New to the Old Whigs' in *Works*, vol. 6.

—Remarks on the Policies of the Allies (1793) *The Works of the Right Honorable Edmund Burke* 16 vols., London: The Rivington Edition, p. 180.

—(1795) *Thoughts and Details on Scarcity*, The Library of Economics and Liberty, Indianapolis, Liberty Fund.

—(1796*a*) *Select Works of Edmund Burke. Letters on a Regicide Peace*, The Library of Economics and Liberty, Indianapolis, Liberty Fund.

—(1796*b*), 'Second Letter on a Regicide Peace', in *Works*, vol. 8, p. 222.

—(1803–27) *A Philosophical Inquiry into the Origin of Our Ideas of the Sublime and Beautiful.* London: The Rivington Edition, p. 235. Gloucester MA: Peter Smith.

—(1972*a*) *On the American Revolution* with an Introduction by Elliott Barkan. Gloucester, MA: Peter Smith.

—(1972*b*) 'On American Taxation' in Elliott Barkan (ed.) *On the American Revolution.* Gloucester, MA: Peter Smith.

—(1975) *On Government, Politics and Society*, edited and with an introduction by B.W. Hill. London: Harvester in conjunction with Fontana, pp. 254–8.

—(1982) *A Vindication of Natural Society* (1757). Ed by Frank N. Pagano. Indianapolis: Liberty Fund.

—(1988) 'A Letter to Richard Burke' in M. Arnold (ed.) *Irish Affairs, Edmund Burke* with a new introduction by Conor Cruise O'Brien. London: The Cresset Library.

—(1993) *Reflections on the Revolution in France*, with an introduction by L.G. Mitchell. Oxford: Oxford University Press.

—(1999) *Speech of Edmund Burke on American Taxation*, vol. 1, The Online Library of Liberty, Indianapolis, Liberty Fund.

Burke, E. and Burke, W. (1777) *An Account of European Settlements in America* vol. 2 6th edn, London. Quoted in Burke, E (1972) *On the American Revolution*. Ed. by Elliott Barkan. Gloucester, MA: Peter Smith.

Burleigh, M. (2008*a*) *Blood and Rage: A Cultural History of Terrorism*, London: Harper Press.

—(2008*b*) 'How to defeat the global Jihadist' *Standpoint*, June 2008, 34–7.

Canavan, F. (1960) *The Political Reason of Edmund Burke*, Durham, NC: Duke University Press.

Chang, J. and Sebag Montefiore, S. (2008) 'Long Night of the Red Star' *Standpoint* June, Issue 1.

Churchill, Sir Winston (1927) 'Consistency in Politics' *Nash's Pall Mall Magazine*, July.

Clayton, J., Blackburn, A. M. and Carroll, T. D. (2006) *Religions, Reasons*, Cambridge: Cambridge University Press.

Constant, B. (2003) *Principles of Politics Applicable to All Governments*, trans. Dennis O'Keeffe, Indianapolis: Liberty Fund.

Conway, D. (2004) *In Defence of the Realm: The Place of Nations in Classical Liberalism*, Aldershot: Ashgate Publishing.

Crick, B. (1993) *In Defence of Politics*, Chicago: University of Chicago Press.

Derrida, J. (1992) *Acts of Literature*. Ed. by Derek Attridge, London: Routledge.

Downie, R. S. (1995) entry on Burke in *The Oxford Companion to Philosophy*. Ed. by Ted Honderich, Oxford /New York: Oxford University Press.

Eastman, M. (1955) *Reflections on the Future of Socialism*, New York: Grosset & Dunlap

Ferguson, Niall (2003) *Empire: How Britain Made the Modern World*, Penguin.

Foucault, M. (1977) *The Archeology of Knowledge*, translated from the French by A.M. Sheridan Smith, London: Tavistock.

Friel, Brian (1990) *Translations*, London: Faber and Faber.

Gandy, C. I. and Stanlis, P. J. (1983) *A Bibliography of Secondary Studies to Burke's Reputation, 1797–1981*, North Carolina: Garland Publishing.

Gottfried, P. (1986) *The Search for Historical Meaning*, Dekalb, IL: Northern Illinois University Press.

Grant, R. (1986) 'Edmund Burke' *The Salisbury Review*, 4(2) (January).

Gray, J. (1998) *False Dawn: The Delusions of Global Capitalism*, London: Granta Books.

Harris, R. (2008). 'De Gaulle Understood that only Nations are Real' *Spectator*, 31st May.

Hayek, A. (2007) *The Road to Serfdom*, multiple editions, University of Chicago Press.

Hill, B. W. (1975) 'Introduction and commentaries' in B. W. Hill (ed.) *Burke, E: On Government, Politics and Society*. London: Harvester in conjunction with Fontana.

Hill, D. (1985) 'Urban studies: Closing minds?' in Dennis O'Keeffe (ed.) *The Wayward Curriculum: A Cause for Parental Concern?* The Social Affairs Unit.

Hughes, R. (1993) *Culture of Complaint*, London: Harvill.

Johnson, P. (1982) *A History of Christianity*, London: Pelican.

—(1984) *A History of the Modern World*, London: Weidenfeld & Nicolson.

—(2008*a*) Institute of Economic Affairs, Hayek Memorial Lecture, 'Freeholds and Property: The Importance of Private Property in Promoting and Securing Liberty', 4 June 2008.

—(2008*b*) 'Roasted on a gridiron for the sake of Green pseudo-conscience' *The Spectator*, 23rd August.

Kirk, R. (1991) Introduction to Stanlis, P. J. *Edmund Burke: The Enlightenment and Revolution*, New Brunswick: Transaction.

Koestler, A. (2006) *Darkness at Noon*, multiple editions. Random House.

Kolakowski, L. (1978) *Main Currents of Marxism*, 3 vols, Oxford: Clarendon.

Laski, H. (1920) *Political Thought in England from Locke to Bentham*, New York, pp. 236–7. [Now available as eBook]

Lecky, W. (1891) *A History of England in the Eighteenth Century*, vol. 5, New York: Longmans, Green and co.

Macaulay, T. B. (2008) *Miscellaneous Writings and Speeches*. E Book, available at: http://www.gutenberg.org/etext/2170

Martin, X. (2001) *Human Nature and the French Revolution*, trans. P. Corcoran, London: Berghahn Press.

Marx, K. (1976) *Capital: A Critique of Political Economy*, vol. 1, Introduced by Ernest Mandel, trans. Ben Fowkes, London: Penguin Books.

McCue, J. (1997) *Edmund Burke and Our Present Discontents*, London: Harvester.

McNamara, J. and O'Keeffe, D. (1988) 'Roots of madness: G. K. Chesterton on the twentieth century' *Encounter* (September/October).

Minogue, K. (2003) 'Christophobia in the West' *New Criterion*, 21(10).

Mitchell, L. G. (1993) 'A Chronology of Edmund Burke', Introduction to *Burke, E: Reflections on the Revolution in France*. Oxford: Oxford University Press.

Morley, J. (1867) *Edmund Burke: A Historical Study*, London: MacMillan.

Morley, J. Burke (2003) *Edmund Burke* University Press of the Pacific.

Namier, Sir Lewis. (1961) *England in the Age of the American Revolution* (2nd edn) London: St Martin's Press. Later republished in New York, 1971.

O'Brien, C. C. (1988) 'Introduction' to Arnold' in M. (ed.) *Irish Affairs, Edmund Burke.* London: The Cresset Library.

—(1997) *Edmund Burke* abridged by Jim McCue, London: Sinclair Stevenson.

—(1990) *The Wayward Elite,* Adam Smith Institute.

—(1998) 'The Philistine trap' in Ralph Segalman (ed.) *Reclaiming the Family.* PWPA.

—(1999) *Political Correctness and Public Finance,* Institute of Economic Affairs.

—(2007) 'History and conscience: On pride, shame and historical reflection' *Quadrant,* September.

Orwell, G. *Nineteen Eighty-Four,* multiple editions.

Pipes, R. (1994) *Russia Under the Bolshevic Regime, 1919–1924,* London, Harvill.

Popper, Sir Karl (1960) *The Poverty of Historicism,* London: Routledge and Kegan Paul.

—(1965) *The Open Society and its Enemies,* vol. 1 (Plato), London: Routledge and Kegan Paul.

Ramsey, P. (1972) *Tudor Economic Problems,* London: Victor Gollancz.

Roberts, A. (2006) *A History of the English-Speaking Peoples since 1900,* London: Weidenfeld and Nicolson.

Rothbard, M. (1958) 'Edmund Burke, Anarchist' *Journal of the History of Ideas,* 19(1), 114–18.

Rousseau, J. J. (1762) *Émile,* published in English and French in the same year; multiple editions since. The full title is *Emile, or On Education.*

Schama, S. (1991) *Citizens: Chronicles of the French Revolution.* Vintage.

Scruton, R. (1994) *Modern Philosophy,* Sinclair Stevenson.

Shanker, A. (1986) 'Where we stand' *New Republic,* 4 November.

Smith, A. (1976) An *Inquiry into the Nature and Causes of the Wealth of Nations.* Ed. by Edwin, M. Cannan. Chicago: University of Chicago Press.

Stanlis, P. J. (1958) *Burke and the Natural Law,* Ann Arbor: University of Michigan Press.

—(1991) *Edmund Burke, the Enlightenment and Revolution,* New Brunswick: Transaction.

Stephen, Sir Leslie (1881) *English Thought in the Eighteenth Century,* vol. 2, London. [Now available published by Kessinger Publishing.]

Taylor, A. J. P. (1976) 'Tory history' in his *Essays in English History*, London: Hamish Hamilton and Pelican, p. 18.

The Listener LVII (1957) 'Burke and the French Revolution', 17 January.

Thomson, D. (1962) *Europe since Napoleon*, London: Longmans.

Todd, William B. (1964) *A Bibliography of Edmund Burke*, London: Rupert Hart-Davis

Index